Mediterranean Cookb

The Complete Easy and Abundant Whole Year Over 199 Recipes for Fast Delicious Meals, Healthy Life, Diet and Weight Loss

Book Description

For having good taste of food, there are few things which must be kept in mind before you start cooking. And out of these, choosing the right kind of ingredients and avoiding the bad content is quite important and most basic one. Talking about the Mediterranean food, the most popular recipes and food items which are made on Mediterranean land are not only healthful but also saves you from horrible weight gains and enormous hotel bills.

Once you go through this book, you will get to know a lot of Mediterranean recipes which can be cooked in everyday routine. Rather you can make the weekly or yearly planning using this guide book. Here is the complete and wide collection of the tastes and cuisines of Mediterranean food. Enjoy the yummiest food stuff that not only serves as the best option for the meal or dessert but also very helpful for the diet conscious people.

Introduction

When it comes to the diet food, you always need a plan – a proper plan. For this purpose, we present you this book that contains the amazing way of doing weekly or yearly planning of making diet food. This book includes 199 different Mediterranean recipes which are all healthy to eat. Each of the recipe has its unique way of cooking and involves high quality ingredients in its making. Particularly, for the beginners, this book includes an extensive variety of the food items ranging from salads to desserts, soups to seafood and so on. You can pick any of your favorite recipes and make it in least time while taking care of your diet and keeping your weight balanced.

The book is arranged in a systematic order with complete info regarding each of the recipe. Along with the photographic aid, the recipes are put in with the proper details of the ingredients and the method of cooking. So, get ready to enjoy the most out of this single book.

CHAPTER #1: TIPS TO BUY FRESH AND HEALTHY INGREDIENTS FOR COOKING

It becomes a big challenge to cook healthy and tasty food. For making good food, choosing best ingredients is also another challenge. But using some tips you can get fresh ingredients. Before purchasing grocery, you need to plan and make a list of things. This will save your time and also help you to save money and get fresh things timely.

You can concern to a nutritionist and get ingredients for the healthy meal and can enjoy your food.

Healthy food to cook

If you are running a home and you have to take care of your family, then you must know how to cook healthy food. You need to get a nutritionist guide and make a diet chart according to. Use fresh ingredients in your food for staying healthy. Use those ingredients in your food which has low fats. Forgetting protein add grains and beans to your meal.

Things to avoid in cooking food

Do not overcook vegetables and do not partially cook grains, cereals, and beans. Take much care while cutting peppers. Use right utensils for cooking food.

How long and easy it to take to cook them

Mediterranean food is easy to cook. If you want to make healthy food for you then choose those vegetables or fruits which are easily available in the season.

Mediterranean food is good for diet and weight loss what facts about that;

Mediterranean food is good for diet and weight loss. This food consists of seafood, fruits, vegetables, and grains. These things will help to fight against cognitive decline, heart diseases diabetes and cancers. These foods will help you in weight loss but you will never lose your energy. Mediterranean food helps you to lower cholesterol level, maintain blood sugar level. It reduces the risk of muscle weakness. This is a fact about Mediterranean food that by including grains and cereals in your diet you can make less expensive food at home. Using the moderate quantity of a red wine in your food gives you many health benefits.

How are popular Mediterranean foods?

Mediterranean food is popular due to its healthy diet. The recipes of Mediterranean food are full of nutrition's. Excessive use of Olives, olive oil, fruits, fresh vegetables, grains, seafood makes the Mediterranean food delicious and healthy. It is popular among those who are health conscious. Mediterranean food represents a culture of many regions that's why it is like in many regions.

Cost to make Mediterranean foods compare to go to restaurants savings

Mediterranean food includes healthy ingredients. If add grains, beans, fruits, and vegetables in your diet and lower meat that you can lower your diet budget. Mediterranean diet does not include those ingredients which are out of range. it makes you healthy. If you compare restaurant's food and homemade Mediterranean food, then you can also compare their cost and impacts on health. So in case of health going to the restaurant will be expensive for your health.

Can the whole family enjoy the Mediterranean food?

Yes, the whole family can easily enjoy the Mediterranean food? Although it has small portions it can be enough for the 6 members. You can get many recipes which are easy enough for the whole family.

CHAPTER#02: HOW TO GET START AND PUT MEDITERRANEAN FOOD IN YOUR ROUTINE EATING DAILY

Mediterranean Meal is a traditional meal and people of many regions love to eat traditional food .But moving from fast food to healthy food is definitely a slow and tough process but eating Mediterranean food means leaving fast food. Although there is no hard rule that must be followed, for the beginner's diet charts can be made by consulting with a nutritionist and you can easily include Mediterranean diet in your daily eating.

Ideas for Mediterranean Meal planning for days, months, weeks and whole year

You can get many ideas on the internet as well as your nutritionist can make a good diet plan for you whether for a year, a month, a weak, or a day. You can search on the internet that which things need to eat and which things need to avoid. What are the things which you can take in less quantity?

How Mediterranean foods are good for diet?

Mediterranean foods are very healthy food. You can use an excess amount of vegetables, fruits, grains, beans, seafood. This will help you to lower your cholesterol level and remove unhealthy food from your life. It gives you a healthy lifestyle.

How Mediterranean food is good for weight loss?

In the Mediterranean foods those ingredients are used which provides you protein, fiber etc. and have immense nutritious value. If you include healthy salads and meals in your food you can easily lose weight. Eating grains, vegetables, and beans instead of red meat will help you in losing weight.

Why people love Mediterranean foods?

People love Mediterranean foods because of its number of health benefits. It is the healthiest food. It's delicious and healthy dishes attract you towards it. It includes fresh ingredients in its dishes which keeps you healthy and fresh.

RECIPE #01: MEDITERRANEAN TUNA ANTIPASTO SALAD

Preparation time: 25 minutes

Servings: 4

Ingredients

- 2 cans of chunks of tuna
- 1 can of beans
- 8 cups of mixed salad greens
- 1 diced red bell pepper,
- Pepper, salt according to taste
- ½ cup of chopped parsley
- ½ cup of chopped onion
- 4 teaspoons of capers
- ½ cup of lemon juice
- 2 teaspoons of chopped rosemary
- 4 tablespoons of olive oil

Directions:

1. Take a bowl and add chunks of tuna, beans, rosemary, chopped bell pepper, chopped onions, half lemon juice, chopped parsley, olive oil, and capers.

2. Sprinkle some pepper. Mix it well.

3. Take another bowl add remaining lemon juice, salt, and some olive oil. Mix green salad in it and put it on the plates. Also, add tuna salad over it and serve it.

Recipe #02: MEDITERRANEAN CUCUMBER SALAD

Preparation time: 10 minutes

Servings: 08

Ingredients:

- 1 pound of tomatoes
- ½ cup of chopped parsley
- ½ cup of red onion
- ¼ cup of lemon juice
- ½ cup of chopped mint
- ½ teaspoon of salt
- 1 pound of Persian cucumber
- 3 tablespoons of olive oil

Directions:

1. Take a bowl and add tomatoes, chopped parsley, chopped onions, chopped mint, and chopped cucumbers. Pour lemon juice and some olive oil over it.

2. Sprinkle some salt over it and place it in the refrigerator before serve.

RECIPE #03: MEDITERRANEAN BARLEY SALAD

Preparation time: 16 minutes

Servings: 06

Ingredients:

- 2 cups of water
- 1 cup of barley
- 7 tomatoes
- 2 tablespoons of olive oil
- 1 tablespoon of balsamic vinegar
- 2 cloves of garlic
- 1 can of black olives
- 1/2 cup of cilantro

Directions:

1. Take a pan add water and barely in it and cook it for 30 minutes.
2. Let it cool.
3. Take a blender and add tomatoes, vinegar, garlic, and olive oil. Make a puree and pour it on the barley. Add chopped cilantro, chopped olives and olive oil. Place it in the refrigerator before serving.

RECIPE #04: MEDITERRANEAN CHICKPEA SALAD

Preparation time: 20 minutes

Servings: 04

Ingredients:

- Pepper according to taste
- 1/2 pint of cherry tomatoes
- 1 tablespoon of Lemon Juice
- 1 chopped cucumber
- 1/4 cup of Olive Oil
- Adobo Seasoning
- 4 ounces of mozzarella cheese
- 2 tablespoons of chopped parsley
- 1/4 chopped red onion
- 1 can of Chick Peas

Directions:

1. Take a bowl add chickpeas, chopped cucumber, quartered tomatoes, crumbled cheese, chopped onions and chopped parsley.

2. Take another bowl add lemon juice, olive oil, and adobo.

3. Pour this seasoning over vegetables and place it in the refrigerator and then serve it.

RECIPE #05: MEDITERRANEAN BROWN RICE SALAD

Preparation time: 15 minutes

Servings: 06

Ingredients:

- 3 cups of water
- 1/4 cup of feta cheese
- 2 cups of brown rice
- 1 cup of green peas
- 1 chopped red bell pepper
- 1/2 cup of raisins
- 1/4 cup of Kalamata olives
- 1/4 cup of chopped onion
- 1/2 cup of vegetable oil
- 2 teaspoons of Dijon mustard
- 1/4 cup of balsamic vinegar
- salt, black pepper according to taste

Directions:

1. Take a pan adds water and rice in it and cook it for 40 minutes.

2. Take a bowl and add chopped bell pepper, raisins, chopped onions, olive, and peas.

3. Take another bowl and add some vegetable oil, mustard, salt and pepper, and vinegar. Place it aside.

4. Put rice in the vegetable mixture and add balsamic dressing over it.

5. Put feta cheese over it and serve it.

RECIPE #06: MEDITERRANEAN ORZO SPINACH SALAD

Preparation time: 15 minutes

Servings: 06

Ingredients:

- 1 tablespoon of lemon juice
- 1 cup of orzo pasta
- 2 tablespoons of olive oil
- 2 cloves of garlic
- 1 pound of ground lamb
- 1 tablespoon of ground coriander
- 4 cups of spinach leaves
- Salt, pepper according to taste
- 3 tomatoes
- 1/4 cup of mint leaves

- 1 lemon zest
- 1/4 cup of parsley
- 1 cup of feta cheese
- 5 chopped green onions

Directions:

1. Take a pot adds some salt and water in it and bring it to boil. Add pasta in it and cook it for 5 minutes.
2. Take a pan add olive oil in it. Put grounded lamb and minced garlic in it. Sprinkle, some salt, pepper, and coriander over it and cook it.
3. Take a bowl and add chopped spinach, tomatoes, some lemon juice, lemon zest, chopped parsley. Chopped green onions and some olive oil. Mix it with the cooked meat and pasta and add cheese over it before serving.

RECIPE #07: MEDITERRANEAN THREE BEAN SALAD

Preparation time: 15 minutes

Servings: 08

Ingredients:

- 1/2 minced onion
- 1 can of white beans

- 2 cloves of garlic
- 1can of red beans
- 2 tablespoons of minced parsley
- 1 tbsp. of lemon juice
- 1/4 cup of olive oil
- Salt, black pepper according to taste
- 1 can of garbanzo beans

Directions:

1. Take a bowl and add white, red and garbanzo beans. Add minced onion, minced garlic, minced parsley, some olive oil, 1 tablespoon lemon juice in it.
2. Sprinkle salt and pepper according to taste.
3. Then serve it.

RECIPE #08: MEDITERRANEAN MEDLEY SALAD

Preparation time: 10 minutes

Servings: 04

Ingredients:

- ½ cup of chopped carrots,

- ½ cup of chopped red onions,
- ½ cup of chopped cucumbers,
- ½ cup of chopped tomatoes,
- ½ cup of chopped bell peppers
- ½ cup of chopped zucchini
- 1/4 cup of Kalamata olives
- 2 ounces of feta cheese
- 1/2 cup of basil leaves
- 1 tbsp. of balsamic vinegar
- 2 tablespoons of olive oil
- Salt, black pepper, according to taste

Directions:

1. Take a bowl and adds, chopped carrots, cucumber, onion, bell peppers, tomatoes, zucchini in it.
2. Then add some sliced olives. Pour some vinegar and olive oil over it.
3. Sprinkle Salt, black pepper, according to taste.
4. Top with crumbled cheese and serve it.

RECIPE #09: MEDITERRANEAN QUINOA SALAD

Preparation time: 15 minutes

Servings: 08

Ingredients:

- 2 cubes of chicken bouillon
- 2 cups of water
- 1 clove of garlic
- 1 diced red onion
- 1 diced green bell pepper
- 2 pieces of chicken breasts
- 1/2 cup of kalamata olives
- 1 cup of quinoa
- 1/4 cup of chopped chives
- 1/2 teaspoon of salt
- 1 tablespoon of balsamic vinegar
- 1 cup of Kalamata olives
- 1/2 cup of feta cheese
- 1/4 cup of olive oil
- 2/3 cup of lemon juice
- 1/4 cup of chopped parsley

Directions:

1. Take a pan adds water and bouillon cubes and a clove of garlic. Then add quinoa to it and cook it for 20 minutes.
2. Take a bowl add cook quinoa, cubes of cooked chicken, diced onion and bell pepper, chopped parsley, chives in it. Sprinkle some salt and pepper. Pour some vinegar, lemon juice and vinegar.
3. Mix it well and serve it.

RECIPE #10: MEDITERRANEAN GREEK SALAD

Preparation time: 10 minutes

Servings: 08

Ingredients:

- 1/2 red onion,
- 2 cups of feta cheese
- 3 sliced cucumbers
- 1 cup of black olives
- 1/3 cup of sun-dried tomatoes
- 3 cups of Roma tomatoes

Directions:

1. Take a bowl and add sliced cucumbers, crumbled cheese, sliced olives, sundried tomatoes, chopped onions and Roma tomatoes.
2. Cover it with the plastic wrapping and place it in the refrigerator before serving.

RECIPE #11: GRILLED MEDITERRANEAN VEGETABLE SANDWICH

Preparation time: 20 minutes

Servings: 06

Ingredients:

- 2 chopped red bell pepper
- 2 mushrooms
- 3 cloves of garlic
- 1 loaf of focaccia bread
- 1 sliced eggplant
- 2 tablespoons of olive oil
- 4 tablespoons of mayonnaise

Directions:

1. Preheat an oven to4000 F.
2. Take strips of eggplant and bell pepper and brush them with some olive oil and roast them for about 25 minutes. Also roast mushroom halves.
3. Take a bowl add mayonnaise and minced garlic in it.

4. Take bread slices. Spread mayonnaise on its halves. Put roasted eggplant's strips, roasted pepper, and roasted mushrooms. Wrap it in a plastic sheet cut it in half and then serves it.

RECIPE #12: MEDITERRANEAN VEGGIE SANDWICH

Preparation time: 10 minutes

Servings: 04

Ingredients:

- 8 slices of tomato bread
- ½ cup of Chopped peppadew pepper
- 1 cup of Guacamole
- 1 cup of feta cheese
- ½ sliced cucumber
- ½ sliced onion
- 4 leaves of Romaine

Directions:

1. Take 4 slices of bread. Spread guacamole over it and arrange a romaine lettuce, cucumber, onion peppadew pepper and feta cheese over it. Put second slices of bread over it.
2. Serve it with desired dips.

RECIPE #13: MEDITERRANEAN GRILLED CHEESE SANDWICH

Preparation time: 10 minutes

Serving: 01

Ingredients:

- 2 slices of white bread
- 1 Tablespoon of olive oil
- 2 oz. of Mozzarella cheese
- 1 oz. of Feta cheese
- 2 cups of spinach
- 4 slices of Roma tomato
- 2 Tablespoon of black olives
- 1 Tablespoon of chopped red onion
- 2 teaspoon of chopped basil
- 1/4 teaspoon of minced garlic
- Black pepper according to taste

Directions:

1. Take a pan add olive oil in it and ad minced garlic and chopped spinach in it. Sauté it for 30 seconds.
2. Then add basil to it.
3. Take the slice of bread and spread feta cheese and mozzarella cheese. Put tomatoes, and spinach mixture. Add chopped onions and olives over it. Sprinkle pepper over it and put another slice over it

RECIPE #14: MEDITERRANEAN VEGGIE PANINI

Preparation time: 10 minutes

Servings: 02

Ingredients:

- 2 tablespoons of Sabra Spreads
- 1/4 cup of black olives
- 1/4 cup of spinach leaves
- 1/4 cup of red peppers
- 2 ciabatta rolls
- 1/2 cup of red onions
- 1/4 cup of feta cheese
- 4 slices of tomato

Directions:

1. Take ciabatta roles and slice it in half. Put Sabra Spreads inside the rolls.
2. Put spinach leaves, red pepper, onion, olives, and slices of tomatoes and put crumbled cheese over it and serve it.

Recipe #15: MEDITERRANEAN FRESH HERBS AND TOMATO SALAD

Preparation time: 15 minutes

Servings: 4-6

Ingredients:

- 1 sliced onion
- 1 cup of chopped parsley
- 2 teaspoon of ground sumac
- 1 tablespoon of lemon
- 1/3 cup of olive oil
- 2 teaspoon of vinegar

- 1 cup of Feta cheese
- 7 sliced tomatoes
- 3 cloves of garlic
- 1 cup of chopped dill
- Salt, pepper according to taste

Directions:

1. Take a bowl and add sliced tomatoes, sliced onions, minced garlic, chopped parsley, and dills.
2. Add vinegar, lemon juice, and olive oil.
3. Sprinkle some salt, pepper, and sumac.
4. Mix it well and put feta cheese over the salad.

RECIPE #16: MEDITERRANEAN TURKEY SANDWICHES

Preparation time: 10 minutes

Servings: 02

Ingredients:

- 1 teaspoon of balsamic vinegar
- 2 leaves of lettuce

- 4 slices of tomatoes
- 2 slices of Swiss cheese
- 1/2 cup of Mayonnaise
- 1/2 teaspoon of Italian seasoning
- 4 slices of bread
- Slices of red onion
- 4 slices of turkey

Directions:

1. Take a bowl adds mayonnaise, Italian seasoning, and vinegar and mix it.
2. Take a slice of bread and spread this mixture over it. Arrange a slice of tomatoes, slices of onions, a slice of turkey and cheese and put another slice of bread over it.
3. Serve it.

RECIPE # 17: GRILLED MEDITERRANEAN VEGETABLE SANDWICHES II

Preparation time: 30 minutes

Servings: 4

Ingredients:

- 2 sliced portabella mushrooms
- 2 cloves of garlic

- 2 sliced zucchini
- 1 eggplant
- 1/2 teaspoon of salt
- 3/4 ciabatta loaf
- 2 cups of baby arugula
- ½ cup of feta cheese
- 2 sliced tomatoes
- 1/4 cup of mayonnaise
- 1/2 teaspoon of lemon juice
- 2 tablespoons of olive oil

Directions:

1. Preheat a grill
2. Take a bowl and add mayonnaise, minced garlic, and some lemon juice.
3. Take mushroom halves, eggplant, and zucchini and brush them with olive oil. Sprinkle salt over it and grill it for 3 minutes. Also, grill bread
4. Spread mayo mixture over the bread and add grilled vegetables over it and also arrange arugula, lettuce leave and feta cheese over the vegetables and put another slice over it.

RECIPE #18: MEDITERRANEAN TUNA SALAD SANDWICH

Preparation time: 5 minutes

Servings: 06

Ingredients:

- 12 ounces of tuna
- 14 ounces of artichoke hearts
- 15 ounces of white beans
- 1/4 cup of pesto
- 2 tablespoons of lemon juice
- 1/4 cup of mayonnaise
- 6 slices of Roman Bread
- 6 leaves of lettuce
- 1/4 teaspoon of black pepper

Directions:

1. Take a bowl add tuna, artichoke, beans, pesto, mayonnaise and lemon juice. Sprinkle black pepper over it.
2. Take a toast and add lettuce leaf over it. Put the tuna mixture over the leave and serve it.

RECIPE # 19: MEDITERRANEAN STYLE SANDWICHES

Preparation time: 15 minutes

Servings: 04

Ingredients:

- Some rocket leaves
- 6 artichoke hearts
- 1/2 cup of green olives
- 1 cup of cheddar cheese
- 2 tablespoons of chopped parsley
- 1/2 cup of red peppers
- 8 slices of multigrain bread
- 1 tablespoon of olive oil

Directions:

1. Take a bowl add cheese, olives, artichoke, parsley, and pepper.
2. Take slices of bread, add arugula leaves and spread the mixture over it. Put other slices over it and serve it.

RECIPE # 20: MEDITERRANEAN MEATBALL SANDWICHES

Preparation time: 20 minutes

Servings: 04

Ingredients:

- tzatziki sauce
- 2 cups of breadcrumbs
- 1 1/2 pounds of ground beef
- 1 eggs
- 1 tablespoon of basil
- 1 clove of garlic
- Cooking spray
- 1 lemon
- 4 spring of onions
- 4 slices of bread
- 1 tablespoon of olive oil
- 2 lettuce leaves,
- lemon wedges
- 1 cup of cherry tomatoes

Directions:

1. Preheat the broiler.
2. Take a bowl add ground meat, egg, minced garlic, chopped basil, lemon zest, lemon juice, and breadcrumbs.
3. Add salt and pepper. Make 18 meatballs and tread it with spring onions and place it on a greased baking tray and cook it for about 10minutes.
4. Place it over the bread and add shredded lettuce and tomato halves. garnish it with the lemon wedge and serve it with tzatziki sauce.

RECIPE # 21: MEDITERRANEAN SANDWICH

Preparation time: 14minutes

Servings: 01

Ingredients:

- 1 tablespoon of Mayonnaise
- 1 hoagie rolls
- 2 tablespoons of olive oil vinaigrette dress
- 2 ounces of cooked chicken
- 3 teaspoons of basil leaves
- 1/4 sliced yellow bell pepper
- 1/3 cup of sliced mushrooms
- 1 slice of red onion
- 2 ounces of fresh mozzarella cheese

Directions:

1. Preheat an oven to 3500.
2. Take a bowl add mayonnaise, vinaigrette dressing, and chopped basil.
3. Spread the mixture onto roll and layer with pepper, sliced mushrooms, pieces of chicken and cheese over the top.

RECIPE # 22: MEDITERRANEAN EGGPLANT SANDWICHES

Preparation time: 35 minutes

Servings: 04

Ingredients:

- 2 sliced tomatoes
- 1/4 cup of parmesan cheese
- 1/2 cup of Mayonnaise
- 1 eggplant
- 4 ciabatta bread
- 4 teaspoons of breadcrumbs with Italian seasoning
- 8 ounces of mozzarella cheese

Directions:

1. Preheat an oven to 425°.
2. Take a baking sheet and spread aluminum foil over it. Place strips of eggplant over it.
3. Take a bowl in which adds mayonnaise and cheese mix it and put it over the eggplant strips. Sprinkle breadcrumbs over it and bake it for 15 minutes.
4. Put mozzarella cheese eggplant and tomatoes on the roll and serve it.

RECIPE #23: MEDITERRANEAN CROCKPOT WILD RICE AND CHICKEN

Preparation time: 10 minutes

Servings: 08

Ingredients:

- Salt, black pepper according to taste
- 1 Cup of brown rice
- 4 chicken drumsticks
- 1 Cup of wild rice
- ½ Cup of olive oil
- 1 Cup of lemon juice
- 4 Cups of water

Directions:

1. Take a bowl add chicken drumsticks in it. Sprinkle salt and black pepper over it. Take a Crockpot and grease it with olive oil.

2. Add wild and brown rice and chicken and then on the top add lemon juice 4 cups of water. Cover it and allow it to cook for several hours.

RECIPE # 24: MEDITERRANEAN RICE SALAD

Preparation time: 15 minutes

Servings: 06

Ingredients:

- 1 cup of white rice
- 3 tablespoons of olive oil
- 3 cups of water
- 1 diced red peppers
- 1 cup of black olives
- 1 green bell pepper
- Plum tomatoes
- 1 pickle spears
- 1 tablespoon of vinegar
- 1 cup of green beans
- 3 cloves of garlic

Directions:

1. Take a pan add olive oil in it. Add rice it and cook it. Pour water in it and bring it to boil.

2. Take a bowl add green beans, chopped olives, roasted pepper, chopped bell pepper chopped tomatoes, pickle and minced garlic. Mix rice in it and pour some olive oil.

3. Place it in the refrigerator and then serve.

RECIPE # 25: MEDITERRANEAN FRIED RICE

Preparation time: 15 minutes

Servings: 04

Ingredients:

- 1 clove of garlic
- 10 ounces of frozen spinach
- 1/2 cup of feta cheese
- 4 ounces of red peppers
- 2 tablespoons of olive oil
- 2 cups of cooked rice
- 6 ounces of marinated artichoke hearts

Directions:

1. Take a skillet add minced garlic in it and sauté it for 2 minutes. Then add cooked rice and frozen spinach in it and cook it for 3 minutes.

2. Add marinated artichoke hearts, roasted pepper and cook for 2 minutes. Before serving top with feta cheese.

RECIPE #26: YELLOW JASMINE RICE

Preparation time: 5 minutes

Servings: 06

Ingredients:

- 2 cloves of garlic
- 2 tablespoons of butter
- 1 tablespoon of turmeric
- 1/8 teaspoon of cinnamon
- 1/4 teaspoon of cumin
- 2 cups of jasmine rice
- 1 bay leaf
- 3 cups of chicken broth

Directions:

1. Take a pot add butter, cumin, garlic, cinnamon, and turmeric. Sauté it for a minute.
2. Add rice to it and toast it. Then add bay leaf and chicken broth in it. Cover it with the lid and allow cooking for 20 minutes.

RECIPE #27: MEDITERRANEAN RICE

Preparation time: 22 minutes

Servings: 2-6

Ingredients:

- 2cups of rice
- 1 chopped onion
- boiling water as per requirement
- 2 tablespoons of olive oil
- 1 clove of garlic, crushed
- 2tablespoons of lemon rind
- black pepper according to taste
- ¼cup of parsley
- 2teaspoons of chicken powder

Directions:

1. Take a pan adds oil and heat it. Add chopped onions and minced garlic in it and sauté it.
2. Add rice and boiling water in the pan. Bring it boil for12 minutes.
3. Add chopped parsley, black pepper, lemon rind, chicken powder and cook it.

RECIPE #28: TAZIKI'S MEDITERRANEAN CAFE'S BASMATI RICE

Preparation time: 5 minutes

Servings: 4-6

Ingredients:

- 3 cups of water
- 2 cups of basmati rice
- 1/2 cup of lemon juice
- 1/2 cup of parsley
- 4 ounces of unsalted butter
- 1/2 cup of lemon juice
- 1 teaspoon of pepper

Directions:

1. Firstly, boil the rice and then put it in the bowl.
2. Add butter, some salt, black pepper, lemon juice and chopped parsley in it.

3. Mix it well and serve it.

RECIPE # 29: MEDITERRANEAN RICE CASSEROLE

Preparation time: 20 minutes

Servings: 04

Ingredients:

- 1/4 cup of olive oil
- 2 cups of brown rice
- 1/4 cup of slivered almonds
- 1 chopped onion
- 1/2 cup of raisins
- 4 cloves of garlic
- 1 tablespoon of lemon juice
- 1/2 cup of chopped parsley
- 2 tablespoons of balsamic vinegar
- 1 Tablespoon of dried dill
- 1 bunch of spinach
- 2 teaspoons of dried thyme
- 3/4 teaspoon of ground allspice
- 1/2 teaspoon of ground cinnamon

- salt, pepper according to taste
- 1/2 teaspoon of paprika

Directions:

1. Preheat an oven to 350oF.
2. Take pot heat oil in it and add chopped onions and minced garlic in it and sauté it.
3. Add paprika, allspice, dried thyme, cinnamon, dried dill, chopped spinach, vinegar, lemon juice, chopped parsley and raisins and cook it for few minutes.
4. Then add rice in it and put the whole mixture into the casserole and sprinkle almonds over it and bake it for 20 minutes.

RECIPE #30: LEBANESE RICE WITH VERMICELLI

Preparation time: 20 minutes

Servings: 4

Ingredients:

- Water as per requirement
- 2 cups of rice
- 1 cup of vermicelli pasta
- 1/2 cup of toasted pine nuts
- Salt according to taste
- 3 tablespoon of olive oil

Directions:

1. Soak the rice in the water for about 20 minutes.
2. Take a cooking pot heat olive oil in it. Add vermicelli to it and cook it. Then add rice to it and cook it. After that add rice to it and sprinkle some salt.
3. Add 3 cups of water and bring it to boil, cover it and cook it for 20 minutes.
4. Before serving sprinkle nuts over it.

RECIPE# 31: MEDITERRANEAN CHICKPEA GRAIN BOWL

Preparation time: 10 minutes

Servings: 1

Ingredients:

- 1/4 cup of microgreens
- 1/2 cup of quinoa

- ½ avocado
- 2 sliced olives
- 1 tablespoon of basil,
- 2 tablespoons of feta cheese,
- 12 cherry tomatoes
- 1/2 cup of chickpeas in Dijon vinaigrette
- 1/3 cup of zucchini noodles
- 1 egg

Directions:

1. Take a bowl and add cooked quinoa, chopped avocado, chickpeas, halved cherry tomatoes, sliced olives, feta cheese, and zucchini noodles. Mix it well and then sprinkle chopped basil and microgreens.
2. Half fry an egg and place at the top of grain bowl and serve it.

RECIPE#32: MEDITERRANEAN GRAIN SALAD

Preparation time: 5 minutes

Servings: 01

Ingredients:

- 1/2 minced shallot
- 1 tablespoon of red-wine vinegar
- 2 teaspoons of olive oil
- 1/3 cup of bulgur
- salt, pepper according to taste
- 1 ounce of goat cheese
- 1/2 cup of parsley
- 1 cup of grape tomatoes

Directions:

1. Take a bowl add bulgur, pinch of salt, and boiling water and place it aside for 30minutes

2. After that drain the bulgur, and put it in the bowl again. Add halved tomatoes, chopped parsley, minced shallot, vinegar and olive oil. Sprinkle salt and black pepper according to taste. Also add crumbled cheese on the top.

RECIPE# 33: MEDITERRANEAN GRAIN BOWLS WITH SALMON

Preparation time: 10 minutes

Servings: 04

Ingredients:

- 4 filets of salmon
- 2 cups of Kamet grain

- ¼ cup of olive oil
- 4 oz. of feta cheese
- salt, black pepper according to taste
- 4 oz. of mozzarella cheese
- 2 cups of cucumber
- 1 cup of Kalamata olives
- 1 sliced avocado
- 2 cups of cherry tomatoes
- ¼ cup of red onion
- basil, dried oregano, and red pepper flakes
- ½ cup of lemon juice

Directions:

1. Preheat an oven.
2. Prepare Kamet grain according to the directions written on the package.
3. Take a baking sheet and place salmon on it. Add olive oil, pepper and salt over it and cook and broil it 7 minutes.
4. Take a bowl add grains, salmon, mozzarella and feta cheese. Add tomatoes, sliced cucumbers, olives, avocado, onion, lemon juice, basil and oregano and pepper flakes. Mix it and serve it.

RECIPE#34: MEDITERRANEAN GRAIN BOWL

Preparation time: 35 minutes

Servings: 04

Ingredients:

- 2 cups of vegetable broth
- 12 ounces of Swiss chard
- 1 cup of water
- 1/2 package of Morningstar Farms® Grillers® Crumbles™
- 1 cup of faro
- 2 tablespoons of olive oil
- 1/3 cup of olives
- 1 sliced onion
- 2 teaspoons of minced garlic
- 1/3 cup of raisins
- 1/2 teaspoon of crushed red pepper
- 2 teaspoons of balsamic vinegar
- 1/2 cup of grape tomatoes

Directions:

1. Take a saucepan and adds faro, broth, and water in it and bring it to boil for 30 minutes.
2. Take a Dutch oven. Add GRILLERS CRUMBLES and water. Cook it for about 4 minutes. Bring it out in a bowl.
3. Take the same oven again and heat oil in it. Sauté onions, garlic, and raisins. add red pepper, crumbles, tomatoes and chard leaves and chard stems,
4. Add vinegar before serving.

RECIPE# 35: MEDITERRANEAN QUINOA BOWLS

Preparation time: 15 minutes

Servings: 04

Ingredients:

- Lemon juice
- 1 clove of garlic
- 1 jar of roasted red peppers
- 1/2 teaspoon of salt
- 1/2 cup of olive oil
- 2 cups of cooked quinoa
- 1/2 cup of almond
- 1 cup of sliced cucumber
- ½ cup of kalamata olives
- ½ cup of feta cheese
- ½ cup red onion
- Pepperoncini
- Hummus
- Chopped herbs

Directions:

1. Take a blender add red pepper, lemon juice, salt, almonds, olive oil, and garlic. Blend it well to make a sauce.
2. Cook quinoa as per the directions, written on a package and after that drain it and return it to the bowl.
3. Mix onions, pepperoncini, hummus, olives, cucumbers, cheese and pepper sauce and serve it.

Recipe# 36: BAKED MEDITERRANEAN CHICKEN AND RICE

Preparation time: 15 minutes

Servings: 4

Ingredients:

- 4 chicken breasts
- 2tablespoons of olive oil
- 1 sliced red onion
- 1 sliced red pepper
- 3cloves of garlic
- 325g grain rice
- 400ml white wine
- 1 carton of pureed tomatoes
- 1cup of black olives

- 8 sun-dried tomatoes
- 1bunch of basil leaves
- Parmesan cheese

Dircctions:

1. Preheat an oven to 180oC.
2. Take chicken breasts and sprinkle pepper and salt over it. In the flameproof casserole heat olive oil and cook chicken in it. Bring out chicken piece and fry onions, red pepper, and garlic in it. Then add rice. And add white wine, olives, sundried tomatoes, pureed tomatoes, and chicken. Cover it and bake it in the oven.
3. Before serving add basil, cheese, and black pepper.

RECIPE# 37: INSTANT POT MEDITERRANEAN TURKEY & RICE

Preparation time: 10 minutes

Servings: 02

Ingredients:

- White Rice 250ml
- 1 Turkey Leg
- 1 Tablespoon of Garlic Puree
- Turkey Stock of 250ml

- 2 Tablespoons of Oregano
- Salt, Pepper according to taste
- 2 Tablespoons of Olive Oil
- 2 Tablespoon of Honey
- 2 Tablespoons of Thyme

Directions:

1. Take a bowl add oregano, honey, salt, garlic, thyme, olive oil and black pepper. Put the mixture over the turkey leg.
2. Take an instant pot, place meat in it. Set the pot on sauté mode and cook it for about3 minutes.
3. Then add stock and set the pot on poultry mode and cook it for 40minutes.
4. Add rice to it and cook it for 10minutes. Then serve it.

RECIPE# 38: STEAMFRESH MEDITERRANEAN VEGETABLE RICE

Preparation time: 10 minutes

Servings: 2

Ingredients:

- steamed zucchini,
- 2 cups of half Cooked Rice
- Red Pepper,
- 1 Grilled eggplant

- 1 sliced Onion,
- 1 tablespoon of Tomato Powder
- 2 tablespoon of Olive Oil
- 1 tablespoon of Oregano
- 1 tablespoon of Basil
- 1 tablespoon of paprika
- 1 tablespoon of Onion Powder
- ½ tablespoon of Garlic Powder
- 4 tablespoons of water

Directions:

1. Take a pan heat olive oil and add onions, red pepper and sauté it.
2. Then add steamed zucchini, grilled eggplant, half cooked rice, tomato powder, paprika, onion and garlic powder, and cook it. Add some water in it to prevent from sticking rice at the end.
3. Before serving sprinkle dried oregano and basil over it.

RECIPE# 39: MEDITERRANEAN RICE PILAF

Preparation time: 35 minutes

Servings: 04

Ingredients:

- 1/2 red bell pepper
- 2 tablespoon of parsley

51

- 1 Tablespoon of Olive Oil
- 1/2 green bell pepper
- ½ chopped red pepper
- 1/2 yellow pepper
- 1 clove of garlic
- 1 chopped onion
- 1 teaspoon of tomato paste
- 1 package of Basmati Rice
- a salt according to taste
- 1 cup of chickpeas
- 1 chopped tomato
- 1/2 teaspoon of paprika

Directions:

1. Take a skillet sauté onion, garlic, and peppers
2. Then add rice, chickpea and tomato paste.
3. Add paprika and salt. Add chopped tomatoes and cook it.
4. Sprinkle chopped parsley over it. And then serve it.

RECIPE# 40: PARSLEY-WHOLE GRAIN SALAD

Preparation time: 15 minutes

Servings: 04

Ingredients:

- 1 cup of chopped parsley
- salt, pepper according to taste
- 3 cups of cooked whole grain

- 2/3cup of sliced scallions
- 3/4 cup of cherry tomatoes
- 2cups of sliced celery
- 1/4 cup of olive oil
- 3 tablespoons of lemon juice

Directions:

1. Take a bowl and add cooked whole grain, sliced scallions, tomatoes halves, parsley, sliced celery, lemon juice, olive oil and sprinkle salt and black pepper mix it well.
2. Place it in the refrigerator and then serve it.

RECIPE#41: MEDITERRANEAN BULGUR WHEAT

Preparation time: 15 minutes

Servings: 04

Ingredients:

- 1 cup of bulgur
- Salt, pepper according to taste
- 2 cups of chicken broth
- 1 tablespoon of olive oil

- 2 cloves of garlic
- 2 stalks of celery
- 6 sun-dried tomatoes
- 1 can of artichoke hearts

Directions:

1. Take a saucepan and bulgur and broth in it and cook it for 15 minutes.
2. Take skillet and heat oil in it. Add celery and onion in it and sauté it for 5 minutes. Then sauté garlic for a minute. Add artichoke hearts, tomatoes in it and sprinkle salt and black pepper and serve it.

Recipe# 42: MEDITERRANEAN CORN SALAD

Preparation time: 5 minutes

Servings:8

Ingredients:

- 1bag of frozen corn
- ½ cup of basil
- 1can of garbanzo beans
- 4ounces of feta cheese
- 1 jar of roasted red peppers

- 1 clove of garlic
- ¼cup of green onion
- 1tablespoon of red wine vinegar
- 1tablespoon of olive oil
- Salt, pepper according to taste.

Directions:

1. Take a bowl and add frozen corn, minced garlic, feta cheese, chopped onions, beans, red pepper.
2. Pout vinegar and olive oil. Mix it well.
3. Sprinkle salt, black pepper, and chopped basil over it and serve it.

RECIPE# 43: MEDITERRANEAN GRILLED CORN

Preparation time: 10 minutes

Servings: 4

Ingredients:

- 1 tablespoon of chopped thyme
- 4 corn ears
- 1 tablespoon of chopped oregano
- Salt according to taste
- 1/4 teaspoon of minced rosemary
- 1 tablespoon of butter

- 1/2 teaspoon of chopped parsley
- 2 tablespoons of feta

Directions:

1. Preheat a grill.
2. Take a bowl add thyme, oregano, parsley, and rosemary. Mix butter in it and sprinkle salt.
3. Brush this mixture over the corn and grill corn for 20 minutes.
4. Add cheese to it before serving.

RECIPE# 44: MEDITERRANEAN BARLEY WITH CHICKPEAS AND ARUGULA

Preparation time: 30 minutes

Servings: 04

Ingredients:

- 1 cup of arugula leaves
- 2 tablespoons of pistachios
- 1 cup of pearl barley
- 1 cup of red bell pepper
- 1 can of chickpeas
- 3 tablespoons of sun-dried tomatoes
- 2 tablespoons of olive oil

- 2 tablespoons of lemon juice
- 1/2 teaspoon of red pepper
- 1 teaspoon of salt

Directions:

1. Firstly, boil barley and then take a bowl add cooked barley, tomatoes, chopped bell peppers, chickpeas and arugula leaves.
2. Add lemon juice, oil, red pepper and sprinkle salt over it. Before serving add chopped pistachios.

RECIPE# 45: MEDITERRANEAN EDAMAME TOSS

Preparation time: 20 minutes

Servings: 4

Ingredients:

- 1 cup of water
- 2 chopped tomatoes
- ½ cup of red onion
- 1 teaspoon of lemon peel
- 2 tablespoons of basil
- ¼ teaspoon of black pepper
- ½ cup of quinoa
- 1 cup of soybeans
- 1 cup of spinach leaves
- 2 tablespoons of olive oil
- 2 tablespoons of lemon juice
- ¼ cup of feta cheese
- ¼ teaspoon of salt

Directions:

1. Take a saucepan adds water and quinoa and bring it to boil for 15 minutes. Then add soybeans and again cook it for 4 minutes.

2. Take a bowl and add quinoa mixture, chopped tomatoes, spinach leaves and chopped onions.

3. Make a mixture of olive oil lemon juice and lemon peel, feta cheese, chopped basil, pepper and some salt and mix it with quinoa mixture. Then serve it.

RECIPE# 46: MEDITERRANEAN CHICKEN WITH ORZO SALAD

Preparation time: 40 minutes

Servings: 04

Ingredients:

- 1 teaspoon of lemon zest
- 2 halved chicken breasts
- 3 tablespoons of olive oil
- ½ teaspoon of ground pepper
- ½ teaspoon of salt

- 2 cups of baby spinach
- 1 cup of chopped tomato
- ¾ cup of whole-wheat orzo
- 1 cup of chopped cucumber
- ¼ cup of chopped red onion
- 2 tablespoons of Kalamata olives
- ¼ cup of feta cheese
- 2 tablespoons of lemon juice
- 2 teaspoons of oregano
- 1 clove of garlic

Directions:

1. Preheat an oven to 425°F.
2. Take chicken breasts and brush oil over it and sprinkle salt and some pepper over it. Also, add lemon zest. And cook in the oven for 25 minutes.
3. Take a saucepan and add water and orzo. Cook it for about 8 minutes.
4. Take a bowl add chopped tomatoes, chopped onions, olives cheese and cooked orzo. Pour some oil, and lemon juice. Add minced garlic, salt and oregano. Mix it well and serve it

RECIPE# 47: GRILLED SUMMER VEGETABLE SALAD

Preparation time: 25 minutes

Servings: 5

Ingredients:

- ½ teaspoon of ground pepper
- 2 ears of corn
- 1 tablespoon of red-wine vinegar
- 2 cups of baby zucchini
- 2 tablespoons of chopped oregano
- 2 bell peppers
- ½ teaspoon of salt
- 3 tablespoons of olive oil

Directions:

1. Preheat a grill.
2. Take a bowl in which adds corn, bell pepper, zucchini, oil, pepper, and salt.
3. Grill the vegetables for 6 minutes. Cut the vegetables and put in the serving dish. Pour vinegar and sprinkle oregano leaves over it.

RECIPE# 48: BALSAMIC BERRY VINAIGRETTE WINTER SALAD

Preparation time: 20 minutes

Servings: 8

Ingredients:

- 2 tablespoons of Greek yogurt
- 1½ teaspoons of olive oil
- 1 clove of garlic
- ⅛ teaspoon of black pepper
- 3 cups of romaine lettuce
- ½ cup of pomegranate seeds
- ½ cup of goat cheese
- ¼ cup of chopped walnuts
- ¼ cup of balsamic vinegar
- 1 tablespoon of strawberry preserves
- 1 teaspoon of Dijon mustard
- ¼ teaspoon of kosher salt
- 3 cups of baby spinach
- 1 cooking apple

Directions:

1. Take a bowl of the vinaigrette and combine yogurt, strawberry preserves, mustard, minced garlic, olive oil, salt, vinegar and black pepper.
2. Take another bowl in which add spinach, sliced apple, cheese, romaine and pomegranate seed. Mix vinaigrette with vegetables and sprinkle chopped walnuts before serving.

RECIPE# 49: WHITE BEAN & VEGGIE SALAD

Preparation time: 10minutes

Servings: 01

Ingredients:

- ¾ cup of cucumbers, cherry tomatoes
- ¼ teaspoon of kosher salt
- 2 cups of salad greens
- ⅓ cup of white beans
- 1 tablespoon of red-wine vinegar
- ½ diced avocado
- 2 teaspoons of olive oil
- Pepper according to taste

Directions:

1. Take a bowl and add chopped cucumber, white beans, salad green, halved tomatoes, diced avocado. Pour olive oil and vinegar.
2. Sprinkle salt and black pepper according to taste and serve it.

RECIPE# 50: SPIRALIZED MEDITERRANEAN CUCUMBER SALAD

Preparation time: 20 minutes

Servings: 6

Ingredients:

- 2 tablespoons of red-wine vinegar
- ½ cup of feta cheese
- ¼ cup of olive oil
- 1 tablespoon of oregano
- ¼ teaspoon of pepper
- ¼ teaspoon of salt
- sliced cucumber
- ½ cup of red onion
- 1 cup of cherry tomatoes
- ¼ cup of Kalamata olives

Directions:

1. Take a bowl and combine vinegar, oil, salt, pepper, and oregano.
2. With the help of vegetable, slices cut cucumber like noodles mix these cucumber noodles with sliced onions, cheese cubes, chopped olive and sprinkle oregano over it.

RECIPE# 51: ORANGE, ANCHOVY & OLIVE SALAD

Preparation time: 30 minutes

Servings: 4

Ingredients:

- 1 tablespoon of lemon juice
- 4 blood oranges
- 3 tablespoons of olive oil
- 1 sliced red onion
- ⅛ teaspoon of ground pepper
- 16 black olives
- 2 teaspoons of fennel fronds
- 6 fillets of anchovy

Directions:

1. Take peeled oranges and cut them into round shape and arrange them on a plate. And keep separates the juice which comes out while cutting.
2. Arrange sliced olives and also add fillets of anchovy.
3. Pour lemon juice and orange juice over the salad. also pour some olive oil

4. Sprinkle salt and black pepper over the salad and mix it.

5. Then serve it.

RECIPE# 52: CORN, ARUGULA & TOMATO SALAD

Preparation time: 20 minutes

Servings: 6

Ingredients:

- Black pepper according to taste
- ¼ teaspoon of salt
- 6 cups of arugula
- 3 tablespoons of red-wine vinegar
- 1½ pints of cherry tomatoes
- 3 tablespoons of minced shallots
- 2 cups of corn kernels
- 6 tablespoons of olive oil

Directions:

1. Take a bowl in which adds shallots and vinegar. Combine them and leave it for 10 minutes.
2. After that add oil to it and mix it. Sprinkle some black pepper and salt.
3. Add chopped arugula, tomatoes halves, and corn. Mix them well and serve it.

RECIPE# 53: BURNT ORANGE & ESCAROLE SALAD

Preparation time: 25 minutes

Servings: 12

Ingredients:

- 2 tablespoons of minced shallot
- 2 sprigs of fresh rosemary
- ½ teaspoon of sea salt
- ¼ cup of honey
- ⅓ cup of olive oil
- 3 sliced oranges
- 2 tablespoons of orange juice
- ⅓ cup of slivered almonds
- 16 cups of torn escarole
- 3 tablespoons of cider vinegar

Directions:

1. Take a saucepan and add chopped rosemary and honey to it. Bring it to boil for 30 minutes.

2. Take a bowl and add minced shallot, vinegar, orange juice, olive oil. Sprinkle salt. And mix it.

3. Strain the honey and again add it to the saucepan and boil it again. Add orange slices and then cook it. Take out slices in the plate. Add remaining mixture to the bowl and add escarole in the bowl. Arrange orange slices over the top and sprinkle chopped almonds before serving.

RECIPE# 54: MEDITERRANEAN TUNA ANTIPASTO SALAD

Preparation time: 25 minutes

Servings: 04

Ingredients:

- Black pepper according to taste
- 2 cans of light tuna
- 1 cup of mixed beans
- 1 diced red bell pepper

- ½ cup of chopped parsley
- ½ cup of red onion
- ½ cup of lemon juice
- 1½ teaspoons of chopped rosemary
- 4 tablespoons of olive oil
- 4 teaspoons of capers
- 8 cups of salad greens
- ¼ teaspoon of salt

Directions:

1. Take a bowl and pour out the jar of mixed beans, add chopped bell pepper, chopped onions, chopped parsley, lemon juice, olive oil, capers, and tuna. And place it aside. Take another bowl in which mix some lemon juice, olive oil, and salad green.
2. Sprinkle some salt and black pepper.
3. Bring out in the plates and serve it with add tuna salad over the top.

RECIPE#55: FENNEL & ORANGE SALAD WITH TOASTED PISTACHIOS

Preparation time: 20 minutes

Servings: 04

Ingredients:

- 1 sliced bulb fennel
- 6 tablespoons of pistachio nuts
- Black pepper according to taste
- 2 sliced navel oranges,
- 1 cup of sliced radishes
- 2 tablespoons of olive oil
- ¼ cup of chopped cilantro
- 2tablespoon of lime juice
- ¼ teaspoon of salt

Directions:

1. Take a bowl and add slices of oranges, sliced radishes, chopped cilantro, and some lime juice. Sprinkle black pepper and salt over it and dish out in a serving plate. Before serving sprinkle chopped nuts over the salad.

RECIPE# 56: CUCUMBER & BLACK-EYED PEA SALAD

Preparation time: 20 minutes

Servings: 06

Ingredients:

- 2 tablespoons of lemon juice
- 3 tablespoons of olive oil
- 2 teaspoons of chopped oregano
- 4 cups of diced cucumbers
- Black pepper according to taste
- 1 can of peas
- ½ cup of feta cheese
- ⅔ cup of red bell pepper
- 2 tablespoons of black olives
- ¼ cup of red onion

Directions:

1. For preparing this salad to take a bowl in which add chopped cucumber, pour the jar of peas, chopped bell pepper, crumbled cheese, chopped onions, chopped olives and pour olive oil and lemon juice over the vegetables and sprinkle salt, black pepper, and chopped oregano over it. Mix it well.
2. Place it in the refrigerator before serving.

RECIPE# 57: WATERCRESS, PISTACHIO & BEET SALAD

Preparation time: 30 minutes

Servings: 06

Ingredients:

- ¼ teaspoon of ground pepper
- 3 tablespoons of olive oil
- 10 cups of watercress
- 1 pound of beets
- 1 sliced fennel bulb
- 4 tablespoons of champagne vinegar
- ¼ cup of chopped pistachios
- 1 tablespoon of maple syrup
- ¼ cup of feta cheese
- Salt according to taste

Directions:

1. Take a saucepan adds water to it and boil it. Fit a steamer basket and put beets over it and cook it for 12 minutes.
2. Take a bowl and add maple syrup and salt and mix cooked beets in it. Place it in the refrigerator for 10 minutes.
3. Mix vinegar, maple syrup, salt, black pepper and olive oil with sliced fennel and watercress.
4. Arrange beets in the bowl and pour pickle liquid. Add cheese and nuts over the top and serve it.

RECIPE#58: MEDITERRANEAN SALAD

Preparation time: 20 minutes

Servings: 04

Ingredients:

- 1 cucumber
- 1 head of romaine lettuce
- ½ cup of chopped tomato
- ½ cup of feta cheese
- 15.5 oz. chickpeas
- ½ cup of parmesan cheese
- ½ sliced red onion
- ½ teaspoon of garlic powder
- 2 tablespoons of red-wine vinegar
- 2 tablespoons of olive oil
- ½ teaspoon of black pepper

Directions:

1. Make the dressing by mixing, garlic powder, olive oil, vinegar and black pepper in a bowl.
2. Take another bowl in which add chopped cucumbers, chopped tomatoes, chopped lettuce, chickpeas, chopped onions, feta cheese and parmesan cheese.
3. Pour the dressing over salad and mix it well. Serve it

RECIPE# 59: WARM ARUGULA BREAD SALAD

Preparation time: 20 minutes

Servings: 06

Ingredients:

- ¾ ounce of Parmesan cheese
- 2 slices of whole-wheat bread
- 3 tablespoons of olive oil
- 1 cup of cherry tomatoes
- 1 tablespoon of minced garlic
- 8 cups of arugula
- ⅛ teaspoon of salt
- 2 tablespoons of balsamic vinegar
- ⅛ teaspoon of black pepper

Directions:

1. Take a skillet and heat olive oil in them. Add cubes of bread and fry it for few minutes. Add tomato halves, chopped arugula in it and cook it for a minute.
2. Add minced garlic to the skillet and slightly cook it.
3. Pour vinegar, sprinkle salt, pepper, and parmesan cheese and dish out in a serving plate.

RECIPE# 60: WATERCRESS & SUGAR SNAP SALAD WITH WARM SESAME-SHALLOT VINAIGRETTE

Preparation time: 25 minutes

Servings: 4

Ingredients:

- 2 bunches of watercress
- ¼ teaspoon of salt
- 8 ounces of sugar snap peas
- 2 teaspoons of sesame oil
- 2 tablespoons of peanut oil
- ½ cup of goat cheese
- 2 tablespoons of rice vinegar
- 4 sliced shallots

Directions:

1. Add water in a pot and bring it boil. Add peas in it and boil it for 30 seconds.
2. Take a bowl add boiled peas and watercress.
3. Take skillet heat peanut oil in it and cook shallots for 15 minutes. Add vinegar, some sesame oil and sprinkle salt. Pour this dressing over the pea mixture. Sprinkle cheese over the tops and serve it.

RECIPE#61: ISLANDER SALAD

Preparation time: 20 minutes

Servings: 06

Ingredients:

- 6 chopped black olives
- 1 sliced red onion
- ½ cup of ricotta salute
- cups of crisp lettuce
- 1 tomato
- 2 tablespoons of tomato juice
- 2 potatoes
- 1 tablespoon of olive oil
- 1 tablespoon of chopped basil
- 1 tablespoon of red-wine vinegar
- 1 tablespoon of capers,
- Salt, pepper according to taste

Directions:

1. Take a bowl and add water and sliced onions in it soak onions for about 10 minutes.
2. After 10 minutes' drain onions and add in a bowl, mix tomatoes halves, chopped basil, caper, chopped olives, lettuce, and boiled cubes of potato and crumble cheese.
3. Add tomato juice, vinegar and olive oil on vegetables and sprinkle black pepper and salt.
4. Mix it well and serve it.

RECIPE#62: SUGAR SNAP PEA SALAD

Preparation time: 25 minutes

Servings: 5

Ingredients:

- Black pepper according to taste
- 4 cups of sugar snap peas
- ½ teaspoon of salt
- 2 tablespoons of lemon juice
- 1 bunch of radishes
- 2 tablespoons of olive oil
- ¼ cup of torn mint
- Aleppo pepper
- ½ cup of goat cheese
- Edible flowers

Directions:

1. Take a bowl in which add snap peas, radishes, chopped or torn mint leaves and crumbled cheese. Sprinkle salt and black pepper according to taste. Pour lemon juice and olive oil over the veggies.
2. Before serving to add Aleppo pepper and edible flowers.
3. Taste it and then serve it.

RECIPE# 63: CHOPPED JICAMA SALAD

Preparation time: 15 minutes

Servings: 4

Ingredients:

- 3 cups of diced jicama
- 2 tablespoons of olive oil
- ¼ cup of chopped basil
- 1 clove of garlic
- ¼ cup of chopped pepperoncini
- ¼ teaspoon of salt
- ¼ cup of chopped sun-dried tomatoes

- ¼ teaspoon of ground pepper

Directions:

1. Take a bowl add minced garlic, some salt, pepper and olive oil. Mix it with the diced jicama, chopped basil, chopped pepperoncini and chopped sun-dried tomatoes.
2. Dish out in a serving bowl and serve it.

RECIPE#64: HONEY LIME FRUIT SALAD

Preparation time: 20 minutes

Servings: 08

Ingredients:

- 2 tablespoons honey
- 2 sliced bananas
- ½ pound of blueberries
- 1/3 cup of pine nuts
- ½ cup of lemon juice
- 1 package of strawberries

Directions:

1. Take a bowl add sliced banana, blueberries, and strawberries.

2. Pour lemon juice and honey over the fruits.

3. Sprinkle chopped pine nuts over it and serves it.

RECIPE#65: PEAR & CHIOGGIA BEET SLAW

Preparation time: 15minutes

Servings: 4

Ingredients:

- 3 cups of shredded beets
- 3 tablespoons of grapeseed oil
- 1 cup of shredded carrots
- 2 tablespoons of lemon juice
- 1 cup of grated pear
- 1 teaspoon of honey
- 1 sliced scallion,
- ¼ teaspoon of salt
- ¼ teaspoon of ground pepper

Directions:

1. Firstly, combine honey grapeseed oil, salt, lemon juice and black pepper in a bowl.

2. Mix beets, shredded carrots, grated pear, and sliced scallion in the mixture.

3. Mix it well and serve it.

RECIPE#66: WARM FAVA BEAN & ESCAROLE SALAD (SCAFATA)

Preparation time: 15 minutes

Servings: 4

Ingredients:

- 2 tablespoons of olive oil
- ¼ cup of chopped basil
- ¼ teaspoon of ground pepper
- 1 cup of fava beans
- ⅛ teaspoon of red pepper
- 1 sliced onion
- 2 tablespoons of olive oil
- 4 cups of chopped escarole
- 1 cup of peas
- 2 cloves of garlic
- ½ teaspoon of salt

Directions:

1. Take a pan and heat olive oil in it. Add garlic, red pepper and onions and sauté it for 3 minutes. Add beans, escarole, and peas. Sprinkle black pepper and salt. And cook it for 3 minutes.
2. Add chopped basil over it before serving.

RECIPE #67: MUSSELS WITH FETA CHEESE (SAGANAKI)

Preparation time: 20 minutes

Servings: 4-6

Ingredients:

- 1 chopped onion
- 2 lbs. of mussels
- 2 tablespoons of olive oil
- 1/2 teaspoon of salt
- 1 glass white wine
- 2 minced garlic cloves
- 1 dash cayenne pepper
- 1 tablespoon of tomato paste
- 1 bunch of chopped parsley
- 2 oz. grated feta cheese

Directions:

1. Preheat an oven to 200° C.
2. Heat olive oil in a pan and add chopped onion in it. Sauté it for few minutes.
3. Remove the shells of mussels and then add it to the pan. Also, add tomato paste and while wine. sprinkle salt over it.
4. Cook it for 5 minutes.

5. Then add cayenne pepper and minced garlic and again cook it for 5 minutes.
6. Dish out the mussels and add feta cheese and sprinkle parsley over it and place it in the oven for few seconds to melt the cheese and then serve it.

RECIPE#68: SEAFOOD PASTA

Preparation time: 40 minutes

Servings: 4-6

Ingredients:

- 300 gr of cleaned squid
- 3 pints of fish stock
- 100 ml of olive oil
- 350 gr of monkfish
- 1 chopped tomato
- 2 chopped cloves of garlic
- ½ teaspoon of paprika
- 300 gr of spaghetti
- 18 tiger prawns

For the Picasa

- 3 Tablespoon of minced parsley
- 2 pureed cloves of garlic

Directions:

1. Take a pan and heat oil in it. Add monkfish and squid in it and cook it for about 5 minutes.
2. Add chopped tomato, paprika and garlic in the pan and cook it for about 5 minutes.
3. Add fish stock and tiger prawns in it, boil it then add pasta and cover the pan with a lid. Cook it for 10 minutes.
4. Take a mortar adds parsley and garlic. make a paste and add to the pan. Dish out the pasta and serve it hot.

RECIPE#69: PRAWNS WITH HONEY SAUCE

Preparation time: 20 minutes

Servings: 02

Ingredients:

- 1 glass of unripe grape wine
- 4 prawns
- 1 glass lemon juice
- 2 tablespoons of olive oil
- 1/2 tablespoon of brown fennel seeds
- 3 tablespoons of honey
- 1 teaspoon of nigella seeds
- 1 grated sour apple

- 1/2 glass of white wine

Directions:

1. Heat oil in the pan sautés prawns in it. Add grated apple, unripe grape wine, lemon juice, and white wine and fennel seeds and cook it.
2. When liquids in the pan dry then add honey to it.
3. Dish out the prawns and sprinkle nigella seeds over it.

RECIPE#70: SEAFOOD PAELLA

Preparation time: 90 minutes

Servings: 4-5

Ingredients:

- 12 prawns
- 1 cup of olive oil
- 1 chopped onion
- 1 cup of white wine vinegar
- 2 chopped tomatoes
- 250 g of oysters
- 250 g of mussels
- 1 cup of shellfish stock

- 250 g of calamari
- 1 sliced lemon
- 5 cloves of garlic
- 2 red bell peppers
- 1 can of cooked peas
- 1 teaspoon of paprika
- 30 threads of saffron
- 4 cups of vegetable stock
- Salt, pepper according to taste
- 2 cups of rice

Directions:

1. Take paella pan and heat olive oil and add prawns in it and cook it and place it aside.
2. Take a blender and heads and shells of prawn, some water and make a pulpy mixture and strain it.
3. Add onions to the pan and sauté it. Then add tomatoes and cook it.
4. For making, sauce Add water, wine vinegar, prawn pulp and shellfish stock in the pan and boil the mixture for about 40 minutes.
5. Take a bowl in which pours this sauce.
6. Take a pan and add calamari and garlic, sauté it and add rice in it. Add sauce, vegetable stock, paprika, salt, black pepper and saffron and cook it. Then add peas, chopped pepper, other shellfish and cooked prawns.
7. Serve it by adding lemon slices over the rice.

RECIPE #71: CUTTLEFISH IN TOMATO SAUCE

Preparation time: 20 minutes

Servings: 4-6

Ingredients:

- 1 chopped onion
- 1/2 bunch of chopped parsley
- 1 kg fresh cuttlefish
- 2 tablespoons of olive oil
- Paste of 3 tomatoes
- 1 glass white wine
- 1 leaf bay
- 1 tablespoon of salt
- ½ tablespoon of pepper.

Directions:

1. Take a pan and add olive oil in it. Add onion in and sauté it.
2. Then add pieces of cuttlefish in it. Then add white wine in it and cook it for about 5 minutes.
3. Then add chopped parsley, a paste of tomato, and some warm water. Sprinkle salt, pepper over it.
4. Then pour it into the bowl and serve it.

RECIPE #72: MARINATED SHRIMP WITH CAPERS AND DILL

Preparation time: 20 minutes

Servings: 4-6

Ingredients:

- 1 lemon
- 7 tablespoons of olive oil
- 2 tablespoons of mustard
- 2 chopped green onions
- 3 tablespoons of Santorini capers
- 2 tablespoons of chopped fresh dill
- 500-gram of uncooked shrimp
- 2 cloves of garlic
- 1 lemon, for garnishing

Directions:

1. Take a pan and add oil in it.
2. Add shrimp to the oil and fry it with pepper and salt
3. Blend the mustard, lemon juice, garlic and dill in a bowl and add oil while mixing.
4. Mix shrimp and also add onions and lemon juice.
5. Keep it in refrigerator
6. Garnish it with lemon and serve it.

RECIPE #73: TARAMOSALATA OR FISH ROE SALAD WITHOUT BREAD

Preparation time: 30 minutes

Servings: 4-6

Ingredients:

- 2 chopped onions
- 1 tablespoon of smoked salmon
- White pepper according to taste
- Lemon juice
- 2 tablespoons of olive oil
- 150 gram of white fish

Directions:

1. Mashed the onions with lemon juice and beat it.
2. Mix the fish roe and salmon and beat it until dissolved.
3. Add the oil gradually
4. Add the lemon juice and pepper as necessary.

RECIPE #74: DIP WITH SEA URCHIN

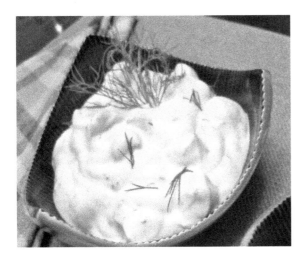

Preparation time: 10 minutes

Servings: 4-6

Ingredients:

- 1 Chopped onion
- White vinegar
- 2 bowls of Greek yogurt
- 1 chopped cucumber
- 1 tablespoon of fresh dill
- 4 cloves of garlic
- 180-gram of sea urchin
- Salt, pepper as required.

Directions:

1. Mix yogurt, sea urchin and vinegar in a bowl and crush it.
2. Add 1 cucumber, cloves of garlic, Onion, dill and mix it.
3. Add pepper and salt as required and keep it in a refrigerator and serve it.

RECIPE# 75: SEA URCHIN RISOTTO

Preparation time: 15 minutes

Servings: 4-6

Ingredients:

- fresh white peppercorns
- 1 chopped onion
- Salt as required
- half cup white wine
- 1 cup rice (Arborio)
- 2 tablespoons of olive oil
- 5 cups of chicken stock
- A half cup of sea urchin.

Directions:

1. Take a pan and add olive oil in it. Fry the onions with white peppercorns and salt.
2. Add rice to it and stir it after that add wine.
3. Include the chicken stock and stir it until it absorbed.
4. Rice is done add sea urchin in risotto and serve it.

RECIPE#76: NICOISE SALAD WITH FRESH SALMON

Preparation time: 30 minutes

Servings: 4

Ingredients:

- salt as required
- 250 grams' beans
- Pepper
- 1 lettuce
- 4 eggs
- 400 grams of salmon fillets
- 2 tablespoons of olives oil
- 250 gram of cherry tomatoes
- 2 medium size potatoes,
- 2 tablespoons of white vinegar
- 1/4 cup of virgin olive oil
- 1 clove of garlic
- Salt, pepper as required

Directions:

1. Take a bowl add the lettuce, cherry, beans, tomatoes, potatoes, and olives.
2. Add the salmon to the mixture.
3. Mix all the ingredients in a bowl and make a fine mixture and pour the mixed ingredients over the salad and serve it.

RECIPE# 77: CALAMARI IN PESTO

Preparation time: 10 minutes

Servings: 6

Ingredients:

Pesto:

- 1 bunch of basil
- 100 grams of pine nuts
- 100 grams of grated parmesan
- 125 ml olive oil

Calamari

- 2 potatoes
- 500 gram of calamari
- 20 ml of Ouzo
- pepper and salt as required

Directions:

1. For pesto mix all the ingredients and make a fine paste and add salt as required.
2. Take a pan and add olive pan and fry calamari after that add Ouzo.
3. Then chopped the potatoes and fry it in oil until the golden brown color appears.
4. Add the pesto to the calamari and fry it and serve it.

RECIPE#78: OCTOPUS IN WINE

Preparation time: 40 minutes

Servings: 4

Ingredients:

- salt as required
- 800-grams of octopus
- 200 grams of chopped onions
- 60 gram of dill
- Black pepper as required
- 300 grams of tomatoes
- 1 tablespoon of tomato paste
- 1 and a half cup of red wine
- 4 tablespoons of olive oil

Directions:

1. Take a pan and add olive oil in it and fry the tentacles with a pinch of salt.
2. Take another pan and add olive oil in it and sauté the onion in it, add the cleaned octopus in it and fry them for almost 3 minutes.
3. Add the paste of tomatoes and pepper into the pan and cook it for few minutes. Then serve it with the bread.

RECIPE#79: PRAWNS AND AVOCADO SALAD

Preparation time: 10 minutes

Servings: 4-6

Ingredients:

- 2 cucumbers
- 4 tablespoons of olive oil
- 8 prawns
- 1 tablespoon of lemon juice
- 1 leave of rocket
- few drops of Tabasco sauce
- 1 teaspoon of spicy mustard
- 1 avocado
- 1 teaspoon of red onion
- 1 lettuce
- 1 teaspoon of parsley

Directions:

1. Take chopped cucumbers and the salad leaves.
2. Mix rocket leaves, avocado, lettuce, mustard, onion, Tabasco sauce, lemon juice, parsley, oil, and prawns in a bowl and serve it.

RECIPE#80: CUTTLEFISH WITH FENNEL AND SPINACH

Preparation time: 15 minutes

Servings: 6

Ingredients:

- 2 cups of spinach
- 1 kilogram of cuttlefish
- 1 cup of sliced fennel
- 2 chopped onions
- 1 cubed tomato
- Pepper
- lemon juice
- 1 cup of olive oil
- 1 sliced onion
- Salt as required.

Directions:

1. Take a pan and add olive oil in it and fry the onions in it.
2. Include the cuttlefish in it and make it golden brown and include almost 3 cups of water in it.
3. Add the tomatoes, salt, spinach, and pepper. Add some water.

4. Cover the pot to make all the ingredients to become soft. After this add the juice of a lemon over the mixture.

5. Serve the meal.

RECIPE#81: CUTTLEFISH WITH SPINACH AND RAISINS

Preparation time: 40 minutes

Servings: 4-6

Ingredients:

- 200 ml wine (red)
- 1 kilogram of spinach
- 1 and a half kilograms of cuttlefish
- 100 grams of brown raisins
- 1 Chopped onion
- 50 gram nuts of pine
- 1 fresh bunch of dill
- 2 tomato's paste
- olive oil as required
- Salt, pepper as required.

Directions:

1. Take a pan and add olive oil to it and deep fry cuttlefish.

2. Add some salt and pepper in the cuttlefish to make it soft. After this add the wine and stir it gently.

3. Add some raisins and allow the mixture to become thickened.

4. In the separate pan add some olive oil and fry the onions and spinach in it. Now add tomatoes paste and pepper as required.

5. Serve the dish with wine sauce and toasted nuts.

RECIPE#82: LOBSTER TAILS

Preparation time: 20 minutes

Servings: 4

Ingredients:

- 2 zucchinis
- 4 tails of lobster
- 1 bunch of chives
- buds of soya
- butter as required
- 1 leek
- 2 chopped carrots
- 200 cc of milk
- Pepper, salt as required

Directions:

1. Fry the lobster tails with salt and pepper and add some wine.

2. Cook the lobster tail for about 10 minutes.

3. Make the sauce by using the cream and chives. Finally, pour the sauce over the tails and serve it.

RECIPE#83: PENNE WITH CUTTLEFISH INK, YOGURT AND SPICES

Preparation time: 20 minutes

Servings: 4-6

Ingredients:

- 250 gram of yogurt
- 500 gram of penne
- 2 dried chopped onions
- 4 tablespoons of chopped parsley
- white wine
- 4 tablespoons of chopped dill
- 3 tablespoons of olive oil

- 12 tomatoes paste
- pepper salt as required
- grated parmesan according to requirement

Directions:

1. Take a pan and add olive oil in it and fry the chopped onions.
2. Soak it in the white wine and boil it.
3. Add the salt, pepper, dill, and yogurt and stir it well and serve it.

RECIPE#84: OCTOPUS STEW WITH FENNEL AND GREEN OLIVES

Preparation time: 30 minutes

Servings: 6

Ingredients:

- Half cup of olive oil
- 3 pounds of octopus
- Half cup of vinegar
- 12 green sliced onions

- 1 cup of red wine
- 1 clove of garlic
- black pepper as required
- 1 bulb of fennel
- seeds of coriander
- 2/3 cup of green olives

Directions:

1. Put the cleaned octopus in a pot with wine and vinegar, add some pepper and coriander seeds for taste and allow it for cooking at lowest heat.
2. Add some water to prevent it from burning.
3. Let it cool and serve it.

RECIPE#85: HERBED MUSSELS AND PASTA

Preparation time: 40 minutes

Servings: 4

Ingredients:

- 1 lemon juice
- 900 grams of mussels

- half cup water
- 1 tablespoon of olive oil
- 2 garlic cloves
- white wine
- 4 tablespoons of butter
- 1 and a half tablespoons of flour
- 1 tablespoon of chopped parsley
- 4 cups of a fettuccine
- salt, pepper as required
- 1 tablespoon of pesto

Directions:

1. Cook the mussels in frying pan with lemon and pepper.
2. In a pan fry the garlic paste. Add the wine and juice of mussels and cook it for some time.
3. Mix the butter and flour in a bowl and add it to the frying pan.
4. Sprinkle the pepper and parsley over the mussels and serve it with the sauce.

RECIPE#86: ARTICHOKES WITH SHRIMPS AND MARJORAM

Preparation time: 10 minutes

Servings: 4-5

Ingredients:

- 2 chopped dry onions
- 12 artichokes
- 2 grated cloves of garlic
- 500 grams of potatoes
- olive oil as per requirement
- 500 grams of shrimps
- Half bunch of chopped parsley
- Pepper, Salt as required
- 2 tablespoons of dry marjoram

Directions:

1. Take a pan and add olive oil in it and fry the chopped onions, garlic, and artichokes.
2. Add some salt and pepper as required add some water and allow the vegetables to boil.
3. Take a pan and add olive oil in it and fry the shrimps with the marjoram. Add the salt and pepper and leave it for about 3 minutes. Sprinkle parsley and serve it.

RECIPE#87: DUBLIN BAY PRAWNS

Preparation time: 30 minutes

Servings: 6

Ingredients:

- 2 sliced onions
- 1 kilogram of prawns

- 2 chopped tomatoes
- Salt, Pepper as required
- 1 chicken cube
- a little brandy
- 1 tablespoon of chopped Parsley
- 1 Cup of water
- 1 cup of olive oil
- 1 tablespoon of sugar

Directions:

1. Take a pan and add olive oil in it and fry the prawns in it.
2. Add the tomato and chicken cube, also add the cup of water to make the prawns boil and become soft. Serve it.

RECIPE #88: GIGANTES (GREEK LIMA BEANS)

Preparation time: 10 minutes

Servings: 8

Ingredients:

- 16 ounce dried beans
- 3 chopped garlic cloves
- 16 ounce of chopped tomatoes
- sea salt
- olive oil
- 1 teaspoon of chopped dill

Directions:

1. Take a pan add the Beans in it for boiling.
2. Pour the boiled beans over the baking dish. Add salt, oil, and garlic and baked for about 2 hours.
3. Then serve it.

RECIPE #89: MARINATED CHICKPEAS

Preparation time: 10 minutes

Servings: 4

Ingredients:

- 15-ounces chickpeas
- 3 tablespoons of olive oil
- 1 tablespoon of chopped oregano
- 1 tablespoon of lemon juice
- 1 teaspoon of chopped parsley
- 1/4 teaspoon of garlic
- 1 tablespoon of lemon zest
- sea salt as required

Directions

1. Take a bowl add chickpeas to it. Add salt, lemon juice parsley, garlic and olive oil. Allow it to marinate for about 5 hours.
2. Fry the chickpeas and serve it.

RECIPE #90: GREEK PASTA WITH TOMATOES AND WHITE BEANS

Preparation time: 10 minutes

Servings: 4

Ingredients:

- 8 ounces of pasta
- 10 ounces of fresh chopped spinach
- a half cup of cheese
- 14.5 ounce of tomatoes
- 19 ounce of beans

Directions:

1. Take water in a pan and boil the pasta.
2. Take another bowl and mix tomatoes and beans add water in it and let them boil.
3. After this add Spanish to it and cook for almost 2 minutes.
4. Serve it with sauce and feta.

RECIPE #91: ESPINACAS CON GARBANZOS (SPINACH WITH GARBANZO BEANS)

Preparation time: 15 minutes

Servings: 4

Ingredients:

- 1 tablespoon of olive oil
- 4 garlic cloves
- half onion
- 10 ounce of spinach
- half teaspoon of cumin
- half teaspoon of salt

Directions:

1. Take a pan and add olive oil in it. Add onion garlic and until turn golden brown.
2. Add Spanish, beans, and cumin along with the salt.
3. Mash beans and allow it to cook for some time.
4. Pour into the plate and serve it.

RECIPE #92: KIDNEY BEAN HEMP HUMMUS

Preparation time: 15minutes

Servings: 12

Ingredients:

- Half cup of lemon juice
- Half cup tahini
- olive oil
- 1 clove of garlic
- 1 teaspoon of salt
- 15 ounce of kidney beans
- 1 teaspoon of cumin

Directions:

1. Add lemon juice and tahini in a blender and make a fine mixture. After this add garlic, cumin, salt and olive oil and make a mixture homogenous.
2. Add beans to the mixture. Also, add hemp seeds and blend them well
3. Then serve it.

RECIPE #93: MEDITERRANEAN BEAN SALAD

Preparation time: 20 mines

Servings: 4

Ingredients:

- 1 can of garbanzo beans
- 1 teaspoon of capers
- a half cup of chopped parsley
- 3 tablespoons of olive oil
- 1 lemon
- 1 can of kidney beans
- 1 cup of chopped onion
- 1, chopped tomato
- Salt to taste

Directions:

1. Take a bowl and add kidney beans, garbanzo beans, lemon juice, tomato, onion, parsley, salt and olive oil and put it in the refrigerator and serve it after 2 or 3 hours.

RECIPE #94: BALELA (CHICKPEA AND BLACK BEAN SALAD)

Preparation time: 15 mines

Servings: 4

Ingredients:

- 15 ounce of garbanzo beans
- 3 tablespoons of olive oil
- Half chopped onion
- half cup chopped parsley
- 1 lemon juice
- 1 garlic clove
- 2 chopped tomatoes,
- Black pepper, salt to taste

Directions:

1. Take a bowl and combine beans, tomatoes, onion, olive oil, parsley, lemon juice salt, and pepper.
2. Allow all the ingredients to give the flavor and then serve it.

RECIPE #95: FAVA BEAN DIP (FOUL MUDAMMAS)

Preparation time: 10 minutes

Servings: 6

Ingredients:

- 1 teaspoon of shout
- 1 can of fava beans
- 1 tablespoon of tahini
- 1 tablespoon of lemon juice
- 2 tablespoons of olive oil
- 1/2 teaspoon of ginger juice
- 1/2 teaspoon of Chile oil
- 1 garlic clove
- 1 teaspoon of vinegar

Directions:

1. Take a blender and add lemon juice, olive oil and vinegar, ginger juice and Chile oil, beans, and tahini and blend it until the mixture become homogenous.
2. Then serve it.

RECIPE# 96: HUMMUS III

Preparation time: 10 minutes

Servings: 16

Ingredients:

- 1/4 cup of lemon juice
- 2 garlic cloves
- 2 cups of garbanzo beans
- 1/3 cup of tahini
- 1 pinch of paprika
- 1 teaspoon of salt
- 1 teaspoon of parsley
- 1 tablespoon of olive oil

Directions:

1. Take a blender and add beans, lemon juice, tahini, and garlic. Make a fine mixture and pour it into the plate.
2. Add the olive oil over the mixture and add paprika and a small amount of parsley and serve it.

RECIPE #97: REAL HUMMUS

Preparation time: 15 minutes

Servings: 20

Ingredients:

- 1 garlic clove
- 1 can of garbanzo beans
- 4 tablespoons of lemon juice
- 2 tablespoons of tahini
- 1 teaspoon of salt, black pepper
- Olive oil as required

Directions

1. Add the garlic, beans and lemon juice in a blender. Make a fine paste.
2. After this adds salt, tahini, and pepper in it blend it well to form the homogenous mixture.
3. Pour it into the serving plate or bowl. Sprinkle pepper as taste and serve it.

RECIPE #98: GREEK GREEN BEANS

Preparation time: 20 minutes

Servings: 8

Ingredients:

- 3/4 cup of olive oil
- 2 cups of onions
- 2 teaspoons of sugar
- 3 chopped tomatoes
- 1 garlic clove
- salt as required

Directions:

1. Take a pan adds olive oil in it, after this adds onions and garlic in it. Fry it until it turns golden brown.
2. Add the beans, sugar, tomatoes, and salt in the garlic and onion paste.
3. Cook it and Pour it into the plate.
4. Then serve it.

RECIPE#99: FASOLAKIA

Preparation: time 10 minutes

Servings: 4-6

Ingredients:

- 1 chopped onion
- 1/2 cup of olive oil
- 1 chopped onion
- 2 teaspoons of garlic powder
- 2 cans of diced tomatoes
- 2 cans of green beans
- 3 potatoes
- 1 tablespoon of parsley flakes
- 2 tablespoons of dried mint
- 1 tablespoon of water
- 1 teaspoon of salt, black pepper

Directions:

1. Preheat an oven to 300oF.
2. Take a Dutch oven and heat olive oil. Add chopped onions, cumin, oregano, and garlic. Sauté it for 2 mines.
3. Then add water, beans, tomatoes, potatoes and bay leaf. Sprinkle pepper and salt and cook it for about 15 minutes.

4. Add olive oil, lemon juice and sprinkle parsley.

RECIPE#100: BOSTON BAKED BEANS

Preparation time: 30 minutes

Servings: 6

Ingredients:

- 1/2-pound bacon
- 2 cups navy beans
- 1 onion, finely diced
- 2 teaspoons salt
- 3 tablespoons molasses
- 1/4 teaspoon ground black pepper
- 1/2 cup ketchup
- 1/4 teaspoon dry mustard
- 1/4 cup brown sugar
- 1 tablespoon Worcestershire sauce

Directions:

1. Soak beans in water 1 night before preparation.
2. Preheat an oven to 325oF.
3. Take a casserole dish and add beans, onions, and bacon.

4. Take a pan add molasses, dry mustard, brown sugar, ketchup, pepper, Worcestershire sauce, and salt. Cook this mixture and pour it over beans. Cover casserole with aluminum foil.
5. Bake it in the oven for 3 hours.

RECIPE#101: BLACK BEAN AND SALSA SOUP

Preparation time: 10 minutes

Servings: 4

Ingredients:

- 1 1/2 cups of vegetable broth
- 2 tablespoons of green onion
- 2 cans of black beans
- 1 cup of chunky salsa
- 4 tablespoons of sour cream
- 1 teaspoon of ground cumin

Directions:

1. Take a blender in which add broth, salsa, cumin, and beans and blend it well.
2. Take a pan in which add the beans mixture and cook it.
3. Add cream and green onions and serve it.

RECIPE #102: BAKED DENVER OMELET

Preparation time: 10 minutes

Servings: 4

Ingredients:

- ½ chopped onion
- Salt, black pepper according to taste
- 2 tablespoons of butter
- 1/2 chopped pepper
- 8 eggs
- 1 cup of cooked ham
- 1/2 cup of Cheddar cheese
- 1/4 cup of milk

Directions:

1. Preheat an oven to 400oF.
2. Take a baking tray and grease it.
3. Take a skillet and heat butter in it and sauté onion in it. Then add cooked ham and cook it for 5 minutes.
4. Take a bowl adds milk and egg in it and beat it. Add ham mixture and cheese. Sprinkle salt and pepper and put the mixture into baking dish and bake it for 25 minutes.

RECIPE#103: BAKED OMELET SQUARES

Preparation time: 15 minutes

Servings: 8

Ingredients:

- 1 chopped onion
- 1/4 cup butter
- 1 1/2 cups of Cheddar cheese
- 1 can of black olives
- 1 can of mushrooms
- 12 eggs
- 1/2 teaspoon of salt, pepper
- 1/2 cup of milk

Directions:

1. Preheat an oven to 4000F.
2. Take a baking tray and grease it.
3. Take a skillet and heat butter in it and sauté onion in it.
4. Make a layer of cheese in a dish and add olives, mushrooms, and onions.
5. Take a bowl and scramble eggs with milk and sprinkle salt and black pepper. Pour it into the dish and bake it for 30 minutes.

RECIPE# 104: DELICIOUS EGG SALAD FOR SANDWICHES

Preparation time: 10 minutes

Servings: 4

Ingredients:

- 1/4 teaspoon of paprika
- 1/2 cup of mayonnaise
- 8 eggs
- 1 teaspoon of mustard
- Salt, pepper according to taste
- 1/4 cup of green onion

Directions:

1. Hard boil eggs and chopped them.
2. Take a bowl and add eggs, mustard, green onions, and mayonnaise.
3. Sprinkle salt, paprika and pepper over.

RECIPE#105: OVEN SCRAMBLED EGGS

Preparation time: 10 minutes

Servings: 12

Ingredients:

- 24 eggs
- 1/2 cup of melted butter
- 1/2 cup of milk
- 1/4 teaspoon of salt

Directions:

1. Preheat an oven to 3500F.
2. Take a baking dish and add melted butter to it.
3. Take a bowl adds eggs, milk, and salt and beat it.
4. Pour beaten eggs into the dish and bake it for 15minutes.

RECIPE #106: MEDITERRANEAN OMELET RECIPE

Preparation time: 10 minutes

Servings: 12

Ingredients:

- 1/4 cup of water
- 1 chopped green onion
- 4 large eggs
- 1/8 teaspoon of salt
- 1 tablespoon of butter
- 1/4 cup of chopped tomato
- 1/4 cup of feta cheese
- Dash pepper

Directions:

1. Take a bowl adds water, pepper, salt, and eggs and blend it.
2. Take a skillet and heat butter in it. Pour the egg mixture into it and cook it. Then add cheese, green onions and tomato and again cook t for few minutes.

RECIPE #107: SPINACH, FETA, AND TOMATO OMELET

Preparation time: 10 minutes

Servings: 4

Ingredients:

- 2 c. of baby spinach
- ½ cup of water
- 2 oz. of feta cheese
- ½ teaspoon of salt

- 8 eggs
- ½ teaspoon of black pepper
- 2 Chopped tomatoes
- 2 tablespoon of butter
- ½ cup of feta cheese

Directions:

1. Preheat an oven to 200oF.
2. Beat eggs in a bowl with some salt, pepper, and water.
3. Heat butter in a pan and add beaten eggs in it.
4. Add spinach, cheese and chopped tomatoes on half of the omelet. Cook it and serve it.

RECIPE#108: MEDITERRANEAN EGG SALAD

Preparation time: 10 minutes

Servings: 6

Ingredients:

- 1 tablespoon of avatar seasoning
- ¼ cup of olive oil
- 1 teaspoon of lemon juice
- ½ cup of olives
- 6 chopped eggs
- 1 tablespoon of minced shallot

- 2 tablespoons of chopped cilantro
- salt, black pepper according to taste
- 1/4 cup of pine nuts

Directions:

1. Combine olive oil, lemon juice, and avatar seasoning.,
2. Add chopped boiled eggs, shallot, nuts olive, and cilantro.
3. Sprinkle pepper and salt and serve it with toasts.

RECIPE #109: MY BIG FAT GREEK OMELET

Preparation time: 10 minutes

Servings: 4

Ingredients:

- 1 teaspoon of dried oregano
- 1 cup of grape tomatoes
- 1/2 teaspoon of salt
- 1/2 cup of feta cheese
- Black pepper, as required
- 8 eggs

- 1 tablespoon of olive oil
- 1 package of frozen spinach

Directions:

1. Combine eggs tomato, spinach, oregano, pepper and salt and beat it well.
2. Heat oil in a skillet and pour egg mixture into skillet and allow it to cook for few minutes then serve it.

RECEPIE#110: HERBED LAMB CUTLETS WITH ROASTED VEGETABLES

Preparation time: 15minutes

Servings: 4

Ingredients:

- 2 peppers
- Olive oil
- 2 corvettes
- 8 lean of lamb
- 1 tablespoon of chopped thyme leaf
- 1 sweet potato
- 1 red onion
- 2 tablespoon of chopped mint leaves

Directions:

1. Heat the oven and put potato, corvettes, onions, and peppers into a tray. Add black pepper.
2. Remove it from oven and place the cutlets on the tray.
3. Bake the cutlets until golden brown. Then serve it.

RECEPIE#111: BACON & BRIE OMELETTE WEDGES WITH SUMMER SALAD

Preparation time: 20 minutes

Servings: 4

Ingredients:

- 1 tablespoon of red vinegar
- A bunch of chives
- 200 grams of smoked lardon
- 6 eggs
- 100 grams of brie
- 1 cucumber
- 2 tablespoon of olive oil
- radish
- 1 tablespoon of Dijon mustard

Directions:

1. Take a pan and add oil to it. Add lardons and fry it.
2. Take a frying pan and add eggs, chives, lardons and black pepper in it. Mix it until homogenous mixture made.
3. Take a mustard, vinegar, cucumber and olive oil in a bowl and serve it.

RECEPIE#112: MEDITERRANEAN CHICKEN TRAY BAKE

Preparation time: 15 minutes

Servings: 4

Ingredients:

- garlic
- cheese
- black olives
- 200 grams of tomatoes
- red peppers
- 1 onion
- 4 chickens
- 2 tablespoon of olive oil

Directions:

1. Add the oil and onions to the baking pot also add some pepper. Add this pot to the oven.
2. Make the hole between the skin and flesh of chicken and add cheese to it. Brush the skin with olive oil.
3. Add the tomatoes to it. Also, add the olives to it.
4. Bake it in the oven and serve it with spicy potatoes.

RECEPIE#113 MEDITERRANEAN VEGETABLES WITH LAMB

Preparation time: 15minutes

Servings: 4

Ingredients:

- 1 tablespoon of olive oil

- Half tablespoon of paprika

- 1 clove of garlic

- 250 grams of lean lamb

- Half tablespoon of ground coriander

- 14 grams of onions

- 2 large sized corvettes

- Vegetable stock

- Half tablespoon of cumin

- red and green pepper

- 250 grams of tomatoes

- coriander leaves

Directions:

1. Take a pan add lamb in it and fry for 3 minutes. After this add the corvettes in it.
2. Add spices and shake it well. After this add pepper and garlic paste and cook for some time.
3. Add the chicken stock. After this add tomatoes and cook for almost 2 minutes. After this add coriander.

RECEPIE#114: SPANISH MEATBALL & BUTTER BEAN STEW

Preparation time: 15 minutes

Servings: 3

Ingredients:

- 1 chopped red onion
- chopped tomatoes
- 1 tablespoon of sweet paprika
- 2 peppers
- Bunch of parsley
- 350g lean pork mince
- 3 crushed garlic cloves
- 2 tablespoons of olive oil

- 400 grams of butter beans

- crusty bread

- 2 tablespoons of caster sugar

Directions:

1. Make the balls of ground pork. Take a pan and add meatballs to it. Fry it for some time.
2. Add the onion and peppers in it. After this add tomatoes, paprika and garlic in it. Cook it for about 15 minutes until all the vegetables become soft.
3. Add the beans in it, after this add sugar and cook for almost 5 minutes.
4. Then serve it.

RECEPIE#115: GARLICKY LAMB WITH PEPPERS & COUSCOUS

Preparation time: 10 minutes

Serving time: 4

Ingredients:

- Packets of couscous
- Olives
- 250 grams of pepper strips
- Parsley

- 4 leg steaks of limbs
- 2 tablespoons of olive oil
- Lemon
- almonds
- 50 gram of garlic butter
- Mint leaves

Directions:

1. Take a pan and melt garlic butter in it. After this add the steaks of lambs in it and fry it.
2. Add the couscous to the mixture after this adds peppers and olives in it.
3. Add the herbs and continue cooking. Add the lemon juice to it.
4. Add the almonds to couscous and serve the lambs.

RECEPIE#116: GREEK LAMB TRAY BAKE

Preparation time: 15 minutes

Servings: 4

Ingredients:

- Breadcrumbs
- 2 potatoes
- Olive oil
- 1 egg
- 2 onions

- 2 corvettes
- Mint
- 250 grams of lamb mince
- Tomatoes

Directions:

1. Heat the breadcrumbs, egg, lamb mince. Add the onion and mint in it.
2. Put it on a tray with potatoes, tomatoes, and corvettes.
3. Bake for about 50 minutes until lamb is soft and then serve it.

RECEPIE#117: SLOW-COOKED MEDITERRANEAN CHICKEN

Preparation time:15 minutes

Servings: 5

Ingredients:

- 1 chicken piece

- salt
- pepper
- olive oil

Directions:

1. Take a pan and add olive oil to it. Add the chicken and salt.
2. Then remove from flame add the pepper.
3. Then serve it.

RECEPIE#118: MEDITERRANEAN CHICKEN WITH EGGPLANT

Preparation time: 50 minutes

Servings: 5

Ingredients:

- 3 tablespoons of olive oil
- 3 eggplant
- pepper
- 2 tablespoons of tomato paste
- 6 boneless chicken breast
- 1 onion

- Salt
- cup of water
- dried oregano

Directions:

1. Take a pan and fry the eggplant,
2. Add the chicken and onion in a pan.
3. Add tomatoes paste and water to it.
4. Pour the mixture over the eggplant. Add oregano, pepper, and salt in it.
5. Bake it in the oven for about 20 minutes.

RECEPIE#119: MEDITERRANEAN MEAT PIES (SFEEHA)

Preparation time: 20 minutes

Servings: 18

Ingredients:

- Chopped onion
- ground cinnamon
- Pine seeds
- Half pound of lamb
- pastry sheets

- lemon juice
- 1-pound beef
- salt
- 1 egg
- pepper

Directions:

1. Take a pan and add beef and lamb in it. Add the chopped onions, cinnamon, salt, and pepper in it. Cook for some time.
2. Add the lemon juice to it.
3. Take a pastry sheet and apply water to it. Add mixture to the pastry sheet. Fold the pastry sheet. Bake it in the oven.

RECEPIE#120: BRAISED CHICKEN WITH MEDITERRANEAN WINE SAUCE

Preparation time: 20 minutes

Servings: 6

Ingredients:

- 6 leg pieces of chicken
- Salt
- 2 tablespoons of unsalted butter
- 3 shallots onions
- olive oil
- 4 cloves of garlic

- 1 cup of Chardonnay wine
- Pepper
- cup of chicken stock
- 1 orange
- green olives

Directions:

1. Marinate the chicken with salt and garlic.
2. Take a pan and add olive oil to it. Add chicken pieces and cook until turn soft.
3. Add shallots, garlic, and salt. Cook for some time. Add the wine.
4. Add orange slices and olives. Cook for some time.
5. Add butter to the chicken and serve it.

RECEPIE#121: GREEK CHICKEN

Preparation time:15 minutes

Servings: 8

Ingredients:

- olive oil
- chopped rosemary
- lemons
- chopped garlic cloves
- chopped thyme
- chopped oregano

- chicken pieces

Directions:

1. Take a bowl mix garlic, olive oil, rosemary, oregano, thyme and lemon juice in it.
2. Put chicken into the mixture and let it marinate for some time.
3. Heat the grill and place the chicken over it.
4. Grill it until a change into golden brown.
5. Then serve it.

RECEPIE#122: GARLICKY GREEK CHICKEN

Preparation time: 20 minutes

Servings: 4

Ingredients:

- olive oil
- 3 cloves of garlic
- half lb. asparagus
- kosher salt

- 1 zucchini
- 1 tablespoon of dried oregano
- lemon Juice
- black pepper
- 1 sliced lemon
- chicken thighs

Directions:

1. Take a bowl add lemon juice, olive oil, garlic, and oregano. Add chicken to it.
2. Put it in the refrigerator.
3. Heat the grill and olive oil in it and put chicken pieces and baked it.
4. When the chicken is ready to add lemon juice.
5. Add chicken to the pan and put the pan in the oven along with the vegetables.
6. When the vegetables are soft remove from oven and serve it.

RECEPIE#123: GREEK ROAST LAMB

Preparation time: 15 minutes

Servings: 8

Ingredients:

- 6 cloves of garlic
- 3 chopped tomato
- 1 leg of lamb
- ½ cup of Lemon juice
- 1 Bunch of oregano
- ½ cup of kalamata olives
- 3 Potatoes
- Olive oil as required

Directions:

1. Add the lemon juice, olive oil in the bowl.
2. Add the herb paste to the lamb piece.
3. Add the potatoes to the dish and bake it. Add the tomatoes, olive, and sauce.
4. Then serve it.

RECEPIE#124: GREEK LAMB BAGUETTE

Preparation time: 15minutes

Serving: 1

Ingredients:

- 2 baguette
- olive oil as required
- 1 tablespoon of oregano
- ½ cup of red vinegar
- 1 lamb piece
- 1shredded lettuce
- red pepper to taste
- ½ cup of feta cheese

Directions:

1. Take a bowl add the vinegar, olive oil, pepper, oregano in it.
2. Dip the lamb piece in the baguette and baked it.
3. Then serve it with.

RECEPIE#125: MEDITERRANEAN PORK CHOPS

Preparation time: 30 minutes

Servings: 4

Ingredients:

- olive oil as required
- 1 cup of chop bone-in pork
- 1 chopped bell pepper
- ½ cup of Pasta Sauce

Directions:

1. Heat the oil in a pan and add pork chops in it.
2. Add green pepper to it. Add in pasta sauce.
3. Cook until pork becomes soft.
4. Then serve it.

RECEPIE#126: MEDITERRANEAN GRILLED PORK CHOPS

Preparation time:10 minutes

Servings: 4

Ingredients:

- 2 teaspoons of dried sage
- 1 tablespoon of rosemary leaves
- 1 tablespoon of dried thyme
- ½ tablespoon of fennel seeds
- half teaspoon white sugar
- bay leaf
- 1 teaspoons salt
- 4 pork ribs
- olive oil as required

Directions:

1. Add the pork chops in it. Mix the herb (rosemary, thyme, bay leaf, sage, fennel seeds) in it. Also add sugar, salt and olive oil. Mix it well. Keep in the refrigerator.
2. Bake it in the oven until they become brown then serve it.

RECEPIE#127: MEDITERRANEAN PORK AND GREENS SALAD

Preparation time: 25 minutes,

Servings: 4

Ingredients:

- pork chops (cut into strips)
- olive oil
- black pepper
- mushrooms
- salt
- salad dressing
- salad greens
- artichoke hearts
- red pepper
- basil leaves

Directions:

1. Heat the oil in the pan adds pork in it. Fry it.

2. Add mushrooms, pepper, and salt and cook it for some time.

3. Add basil leaves, artichoke hearts and add the remaining mushrooms to it.

4. Cook it and serve it.

RECEPIE#128: TUSCAN PORK AND BEAN SALAD

Preparation time: 15 minutes

Servings: 4

Ingredients:

- pork chops
- cannellini beans
- pimiento strips
- tomatoes
- artichoke hearts
- green onions
- salad dressing
- parmesan cheese

Directions:

1. Add the cheese, salt, and pepper in a bowl. Mix the pork in it

2. Bake the pork and serve it with the cheese.

RECEPIE#129: GROUND BEEF SALAD

Preparation time: 20 minutes

Servings: 4

Ingredients:

- white rice
- ground beef
- garlic cloves
- paprika
- tomatoes
- 1 onions
- black-eyed peas
- black olives
- olive oil

Directions

1. Boil the rice, fry the skillet by adding garlic paste.
2. Add the meat to it. Add the onions, peas and tomatoes in it.
3. Add the olives and paprika to it.

4. Mix it in the bowl the meat and rice and serve it.

RECEPIE#130: MEDITERRANEAN GRILLED STEAK

Preparation time: 20 minutes

Servings: 4

Ingredients:

- ½ cup of wishbone
- 2 garlic cloves
- 1sprigrosemary
- 1 and a half pounds' steak

Directions:

1. Firstly, marinate the steak with garlic, paste, rosemary and wishbone.
2. Pour the mixture into the baking dish and bake it for about 15 minutes.
3. Then serve it.

RECEPIE#131: MEDITERRANEAN GARLIC HERB BEEF SKEWERS

Preparation time: 20 minutes

Servings: 4

Ingredients:

- ½ cup of Chopped herbs
- half cup white wine
- 1 pound of beef steak
- black pepper as required
- mushrooms
- 1 onion
- salt as required
- ½ cup of olive oil

Directions

1. Thread the skewer with the mushroom and meat.
2. Apply olive oil on it.
3. Keep it in the refrigerator.
4. Keep it in the oven and baked it until golden brown.

RECEPIE#132: GRILLED CHICKEN BREAST

Preparation time: 20 minutes,

Servings: 4

Ingredients:

- 3 tablespoons of lemon juice
- 4 chicken breast
- 3 tablespoons of olive oil
- 3 cloves of garlic
- ½ teaspoon of salt
- 3 tablespoons of parsley
- ½ teaspoon of dried oregano
- 1 teaspoon of paprika
- ½ teaspoon of pepper

Directions:

1. Take a bowl in which adds olive oil, paprika, garlic, oregano, parsley and lemon juice.
2. Take pieces of chicken pour this mixture over it and sprinkle pepper and salt over it.
3. Leave it for 20minutes.then grill it for 5 minutes.

RECIPE#133: MEDITERRANEAN WHOLE WHEAT PIZZA

Preparation time: 15 minutes

Servings: 4

Ingredients:

- 2 tablespoons of sliced pepperoncini
- feta cheese
- 2 tablespoons of chopped olives (Kalamata's)
- a half cup of artichoke hearts
- 1 pizza crust (wheat)
- 1 jar of basil pesto

Directions:

1. Spread pizza crust and spread the basil pesto over it.
2. Add the artichoke heart over pizza, also add kalamata, olives, and pepperoncini.
3. Baked into the oven at a suitable temperature

RECIPE# 134: GARDEN VEGGIE PIZZA SQUARES

Preparation time: 5 minutes

Servings: 4

Ingredients:

- Packet crescent rolls
- a packet of Ranch-style
- a half cup of chopped fresh broccoli
- a half cup of red peppers
- 1 packet of cream cheese
- a half cup of green pepper
- a half cup of green onions
- 2 chopped carrots

Directions:

1. Spread the crescent rolls on the large baking sheet. Bake it in the oven until golden brown.
2. Take a bowl mix cream and dressing mix together.
3. Pour this mixture over the baked crust of crescent roll. Add the red peppers, broccoli, green onions, and carrots.
4. Put it in the refrigerator and then serve it.

RECIPE#135: MEDITERRANEAN PESTO PIZZA

Preparation time: 10 minutes

Servings: 2

Ingredients:

- 2 tablespoons of pesto
- 8 Kalamata olives
- Greek flatbreads (pita)
- 2 chopped tomatoes
- feta cheese

Directions:

1. Take a pita and spread pesto over it. Add tomatoes, cheese, olives.
2. Put each pita on the baking sheet.
3. Bake it in the oven for about 8 minutes.
4. Then serve it.

RECIPE#136: AMAZING WHOLE WHEAT PIZZA CRUST

Preparation time: 25 minutes

Servings:4-6

Ingredients:

- 1 teaspoon of sugar
- 1 and a half cup of warm water
- 1 tablespoon of dry yeast

- 2 cups of wheat flour
- 1 teaspoon of salt
- 1 tablespoon of olive oil
- 1 and a half cup of flour

Directions:

1. Take a bowl adds sugar and dissolve it. Add the small amount of yeast. Add olive oil to the mixture.
2. After this add wheat flour in it. Pour this dough into another bowl with oil on the surface. Leave it for some time. After this divide the dough into two pieces and add cheese, meats, and vegetables as a topping.
3. Bake it in the oven for about 20 minutes.

RECIPE#137: VEGETARIAN SAUSAGE SUBSTITUTE PIZZA

Preparation time: 15 minutes

Serving: 6-8

Ingredients:

- Cup of vegan pesto

- olive oil
- vegetarian sausages
- 11-inch of pizza crust
- Can of chopped artichoke hearts
- Cup of grated mozzarella cheese
- tomato sauce

Directions:

1. 2. Take a pan and add vegetables and sausages in it. Cook for some time until the color change.
2. Take a pre-baked pizza crust and add tomatoes, cheese and the vegetables and sausages over it.
3. Bake it for 15 minutes.
4. Then serve it.

RECIPE#138: GRILLED EGGPLANT AND FRESH BASIL VEGETARIAN PIZZA

Preparation time: 10 minutes

Servings: 8

Ingredients:

- eggplant
- Basil leaves
- olive oil

- Cup of pizza sauce
- Cup of grated mozzarella cheese
- Pizza dough

Directions:

1. Take eggplant and apply olive oil over it on the grill pan.
2. Add pizza sauces on the dough. Add the slices of eggplant over it.
3. Spread a layer of pizza sauce on top of the dough.
4. After this add basil leaves and sprinkle over the pizza. Also, add grated cheese.
5. Bake it in the oven for about 15 minutes and serve it.

RECIPE#139: VEGETARIAN BARBECUE CHICKEN WING PIZZA RECIPE

Preparation time: 10 minutes

Servings: 4

Ingredients:

- Sauce.
- pizza crust
- 1 tablespoon of chopped cilantro
- Packet of "chicken" wings
- black pepper

- 1 lime wedge
- mozzarella cheese
- red pepper
- red onion

Directions:

1. Add sauce (barbecue) on the pizza crust. Add onions, cheese and chicken wings over it. Also, add red pepper as taste.
2. Bake into the oven for about 15 minutes until crispy and golden.
3. Then serve it with sprinkle pepper or chopped lime wedge over it.

RECIPE#140: A PIZZA WITH FRUIT

Preparation time: 20 minutes

Servings: 12

Ingredients:

- frozen blueberries
- 2 kiwifruit
- cream cheese
- cup of sugar
- cup of apple jelly
- sugar cookies
- half teaspoon of vanilla

- fresh strawberries

Directions:

1. Make dough in an oven and take a bowl and add cheese, vanilla, and sugar in it. Blend the mixture.
2. Pour this mixture over the pizza crust.
3. Mix the fruit and jelly and chilled it in the refrigerator.
4. Then serve it.

RECIPE#141: OLIVE FLATBREAD (FOCACCIA)

Preparation time: 15 minutes

Servings: 4

Ingredients:

1. 450 grams of flour
2. olive oil
3. warm water
4. 2 teaspoons of dried yeast
5. 1 and a half teaspoon of salt
6. Chopped black olives
7. sea salt as required.

Directions:

1. Take a bowl and add yeast and flour in it. Mix it well.

2. After the added water, oil and salt in it. Mix the mixture well.

3. Leave it for some time. After this add olives and mix it again. Leave it for some time.

4. After this, spread the dough over the baking sheet.

5. Bake it for about 45 minutes.

6. Then serve it.

RECIPE#142: GREEK PIZZA

Preparation time: 20 minutes

Servings: 4

Ingredients:

- pizza crusts
- 2 oz. of cheese
- 4 tablespoons of olive oil
- Crushed oregano leaves (dried)
- cup of kalamata
- fresh leaves of spinach
- 1 chopped tomatoes
- 2 chopped garlic cloves

Directions:

1. Take a pan add olive oil in it, add the spinach, garlic, and oregano in it and cook for about 2 minutes.
2. Take a baking sheet and put a pizza crust over it. Pour the Spanish mixture over it. Put the tomatoes, olives, and cheese over it and baked it for 15 minutes.
3. Then serve it.

RECIPE#143: MEDITERRANEAN PESTO PIZZA

Preparation time: 15 minutes

Servings 2

Ingredients:

- olives
- 2 tablespoons of pesto
- 2 chopped tomatoes
- 1 Cup of feta cheese
- 2 pieces of flatbread (pita)

Direction:

1. Take bread and spread the pesto over it. Add the cheese, tomatoes, and olives on it.
2. Bake it in the oven for about 8 minutes and then serve it.

RECIPE#144: GRILLED MEDITERRANEAN GREEK PIZZA WITH SUNDRIED TOMATO CHICKEN SAUSAGE

Preparation time: 20 minutes

Servings: 4

Ingredients:

- Italian cheese
- Crumbles of feta cheese crumbles
- 1 and a half teaspoon of dried oregano
- olive oil of garlic
- pizza crust
- dried tomatoes
- pizza sauce

Directions:

1. Take a baked pizza crust and apply olive oil on both sides. Place the pizza crust on the grill.
2. After some time change the side of crust and spread sauce on the baked side. Add the oregano and cheese over it.
3. Grill it for 10 minutes and baked it in the oven.
4. Apply pesto to the pita and add cheese, olive, and tomatoes over it. Bake it for 8 minutes.
5. Then serve it.

RECIPE#145: MEDITERRANEAN BLACK OLIVE BREAD

Preparation time: 20 minutes

Servings: 15

Ingredients:

- 1 teaspoon of salt
- 2 teaspoons of yeast
- 3 tablespoons of olive oil
- 1 tablespoon of cornmeal
- 3 cups of bread flour
- Half cup of chopped black olives
- 2 tablespoons of white sugar
- Warm water

Directions:

1. Take a bowl, mix the yeast, flour, olives, and water in it. Leave it for some time.
2. Spread the dough over the board. Put a water pan in the oven.
3. Take out the loaf and apply some oil over it and sprinkle cornmeal.
4. Bake it until turn golden brown.
5. Then serve it.

RECIPE#146: ROCCO'S OLIVE BREAD

Preparation time: 5 minutes

Servings: 14

Ingredients:

- Water
- 1 and a half tablespoon of butter
- black olives
- 3 cups of bread flour
- 1 and a half tablespoon of brown sugar
- Garlic salt
- 2 teaspoons of yeast

Directions:

1. Take a bowl and add bread flour, brown sugar, salt, yeast, black olives, butter, and water. Mix all the ingredients well.
2. Bake it then serves it.

RECIPE#147: CHEESY BREAD

Preparation time: 15 minutes

Servings: 12

Ingredients:

- 1 ounce of dressing
- 2 baguette
- 3 cups of cheese
- 2 ounces of chopped black olives
- 1 cup of mayonnaise
- 4 chopped green onions

Direction:

1. Take a bowl and add cheese, mayonnaise, dressing mix, olives and onions in it.
2. Spread the mixture over baguette slice. Arrange them in the baking dish.
3. Bake it in the oven and then serve it.

RECIPE#148: BAZLAMA - TURKISH FLAT BREAD

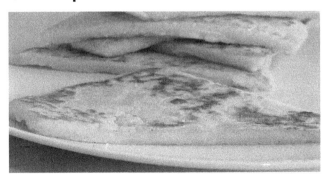

Preparation time: 30minutes

Servings: 8

Ingredients:

- dry yeast
- white sugar
- 1 tablespoon of salt
- 4 cups of flour
- 1 and a half cup of warm water
- Half cup of yogurt
- 4 cups of flour
- 1 and a half cup of warm water
- warm water

Direction:

1. Take a bowl dissolve sugar, salt, and yeast in water. Add the yogurt and water in flour.
2. The dough becomes soft. Make balls of the dough. Cover it for some time.
3. Heat the iron griddle. Place the dough over it and bake until golden brown.
4. Make the other ball and repeat the process.
5. Then serve it.

RECIPE#149: PEPPY'S PITA BREAD

Preparation time: 30 minutes

Servings: 8

Ingredients:

- warm water
- 1 cup of flour
- 1 teaspoon of salt
- 1 tablespoon of vegetable oil
- 1 and a half teaspoon of sugar
- 1 and a half teaspoon of dry yeast

Directions:

1. Make dough.
2. Spread the dough on the board. Make it thin. Cut into 8 equal size pieces. Make a ball of each slice.
3. Bake it in the oven until golden brown.
4. Make the pitas soft by covering it with a plastic sheet and store it for some days.

RECIPE#150: CHEF JOHN'S PITA BREAD

Preparation time: 30 minutes

Servings: 8

Ingredients:

- yeast

- warm water
- 1 and a half tablespoon of olive oil
- 1 cup of flour
- 1 teaspoon of salt

Directions:

1. Take a bowl add water and yeast in it. Add a cup of the floor. Mix it well.
2. Add olive oil, salt in it.
3. Make small balls of the mixture.
4. Cover the balls with the oily plastic.
5. Cover dough balls with lightly oiled plastic wrap.
6. Make a thin layer of dough. Put it over the hot skillet. Add the mixture.
7. Bake it and serve it.

RECIPE#151: GARLIC CHEESE FLATBREAD

Preparation time: 40 minutes

Servings: 8

Ingredients:

- dry yeast
- lukewarm water

- salt
- white sugar
- bread flour
- garlic powder
- olive oil
- butter or margarine
- mozzarella cheese
- Parmesan cheese

Directions:

1. Take a small bowl, add yeast to the water.
2. Take another bowl and add salt, sugar, flour in it. Pour the mixture into it.
3. Beat it well and make a fine mixture.
4. Take a sheet and spread the dough over it.
5. Add the cheese and garlic powder to the mixture. And spread over the dough.
6. Bake it in the oven for about 20 minutes and then serve it.

RECIPE#152: FRENCH BREAD ROLLS

Preparation timc: 20 minutes

Serving: 10

Ingredients:

- warm water
- 4 cups of bread flour
- 2 tablespoons of sugar
- 1 tablespoon of yeast

- 1 teaspoon salt
- 2 tablespoons of vegetable oil

Directions:

1. Take a bowl and add water and yeast to it.
2. Add the oil and salt to it. Stir the flour in a bowl and add the mixture to it.
3. Cover the bowl with the plastic cover.
4. Make the dough flat. Divide it into 16 parts and make round balls.
5. Bake it until the color change. Then serve it.

RECIPE#153: SWEET HONEY FRENCH BREAD

Preparation time: 5 minutes

Servings: 12

Ingredients:

- 2 teaspoons of olive oil
- honey
- 2 teaspoons of honey
- white sugar
- water

- bread flour 2 cups
- salt
- 1 and a half teaspoon of active dry yeast

Direction:

1. Take a bowl mix flour, sugar, honey and yeast, olive oil and water to a boil.
2. Bake it in the oven and then serve it.

RECIPE#154: FRENCH BAGUETTES

Preparation time: 15 minutes

Servings: 12

Ingredients:

- 1 Cup of water
- 1 and a half teaspoon of yeast
- 2 cups of bread flour
- white sugar
- salt
- water
- egg yolk

Direction:

1. Take a bowl add flour, salt, sugar, and yeast in it.

2. Take flour spread it on the board. Cut the dough in half.

3. Cover the dough with the plastic cover.

4. Mix the egg and water into the dough.

5. Bake it in the oven and then serve it.

RECIPE#155: MUSSELS STUFFED WITH RICE

Preparation time: 20 minutes

Servings: 8

Ingredients:

- 8 large size mussels
- 1 chopped onion
- Pine seeds
- Olive oil as require
- 1 tablespoon of chopped parsley
- Pepper, Salt as required
- 1 cup of pilaf rice

Direction:

1. Keep the mussels in pan for boiling.
2. Take a pan and add olive oil and fry the onion.
3. Add the pine seeds, chopped parsley and rice in the pan and fill the whole mixture in the shells of mussels.
4. Now mussels are put in a hot pan with olive oil and little amount of water so that rice become softens. Then Serve it.

RECIPE#156: STUFFED SQUID

Preparation time: 30 minutes

Servings: 4-6

Ingredients:

- 1-kilogram squid
- 1 cup rice
- 1 tablespoon sugar
- 1 and a half cup olive oil
- cinnamon
- 1 tomato
- Chopped parsley
- 2 chopped onions
- Pepper, salt as required

Directions:

1. Take a pan and add oil to it and fry the chopped onions.
2. After this add the tentacles, and rice, also add some pepper and salt as required.
3. After this add the sugar and the cinnamon.

4. Add some wine. When the mixture dried add the chopped parsley.

5. Fill squid with material and put in the pan also add tomatoes and stir it gently.

6. After this pour the squid in the plate and serve it.

RECIPE#157: SALTED ROE SALAD WITH CELERY

Preparation time: 15 minutes

Servings: 2

Ingredients:

- 50 gram of salted roe
- 2 chopped stalks celery
- 200 grams of chopped tomatoes
- olive oil
- salt as required
- ground pepper
- 1 lemon juice
- 4 slices of yeast bread.
- Rye

Directions:

1. Take a bowl in which adds chopped celery, tomatoes and salted roe.
2. Mix the lemon juice, olive oil and pour the mixture on the slice of bread or rye.
3. Sprinkle pepper on the bread and add olive oil.

RECIPE #158: PRAWNS WITH TOMATO AND BASIL PESTO

Preparation time: 15 minutes

Servings: 4-6

Ingredients:

- 18 pieces of prawns
- 18 chopped tomatoes
- Cheese
- 3 tablespoons olive oil
- mint leaves
- half glass of wine
- salt as required
- pesto sauce ingredients
- olive oil
- 1 cup of pine seeds
- 1 cup of chopped parsley leaves

- 1 cup of cheese (parmesan)
- 2 spoons of vinegar
- 1 chopped garlic clove
- salt as required
- grounded pepper

Directions:

1. Take the pan and add some olive oil in it and fry the prawns and sprinkle some salt.
2. Add tomatoes, wine, and pepper and cooked it well.
3. To make the pesto, blend the pine seeds and oil in the blender after this add the garlic and parsley leaves and blend it more to make the fine mixture.
4. After this add a small amount of vinegar and add water to make it thin. Serve the dish with the sauce.

RECIPE #159: GRILLED SQUID STUFFED WITH FETA CHEESE

Preparation time: 30 minutes

Servings: 4

Ingredients:

- 4 squids
- 8 pieces of cheese

- 4 marjoram leaves
- 2 crushed garlic cloves.
- Salt, Pepper as required
- Olive oil
- Lemon for garnishing.

Directions:

1. Take a pan and add some olive oil in it. Add two garlic cloves and cheese add salt and pepper and fill the mixture with the clean squid.

RECIPE# 160: PEARL BARLEY WITH SHRIMPS AND SAFFRON

Preparation time: 30 minutes

Servings: 2-4

Ingredients:

- 1chopped tomato
- 8 shrimps

- 2chopped onions
- 2 cups barley
- salt as required
- 1 cup of boiled beans
- 2 spoons chopped parsley
- sunflower oil
- saffron as per requirement
- juice of a lemon
- pepper as per requirement
- olive oil as per requirement

Directions:

2. Boil the barley with some salt in it.
3. Soak the saffron in the water when it leafs its color mix the olive oil and lemon juice in it also add some salt and pepper.
4. Take a pan and add olive oil in it cut the tomatoes into small pieces and add into the warm olive oil.
5. After that mix the barley with the beans and shrimps and serve.

RECIPE #161: BRUSCHETTA WITH SHRIMP AND PARSLEY DIP

Preparation time: 15 minutes

Servings: 4

Ingredients:

- 8 slices of bread
- 200 grams of cheese
- Bunch of parsley
- mint leaves
- 6 tablespoons of olive oil
- 16 shrimps boiled

Directions:

1. Blend the mint, olive oil, pepper, parsley and salt and make a mixture.
2. Bake the bread slice.
3. Pour the mixture over the bread slice and add shrimps and serve it.

RECIPE#162: BATTERED FRIED SHRIMP AND SUN-DRIED TOMATO CREAM

Preparation time: 30 minutes

Servings: 16 pieces

Ingredients:

- 16 shrimps
- 100 grams of flour
- 100 grams of corn flour
- 100 ml of soda water
- 2 tablespoons of herbs like dill, parsley, and basil.
- Salt as required
- Pepper.

    For the ouzo tomato cream

- 100 ml of mayonnaise
- 2 dried tomatoes
- 1 chopped onion
- 1 tablespoon of chopped parsley
- Pepper, salt as required
- sunflower oil as required

Directions:

1. Prepare the mash with the flour, soda, cornflower, and salt.
2. Dunk the clean shrimp in the mash and fry it in oil.
3. Prepare the cream like mixture by using the tomatoes and mayonnaise and salt and pepper
4. Serve the shrimps with the cream.

REECIPE#163: SPANISH CRAB SOUP (SOPA DE CANGREJO)

Preparation time: 30 minutes

Servings: 4-6

Ingredients:

- 1chopped onion
- 2 tablespoons of ham
- 3 cups of fish stock
- 2 tablespoons of olive oil
- 4 tomatoes
- a half cup of crabmeat
- 4 oz. peeled shrimps
- 3 tablespoons of cream

Directions:

1. Take a pan and add some olive oil in it and add the chopped onions in it. Add the ham and tomatoes and stock of fish.
2. Blend the mixture and pour it into the pan and add the shrimps and meat. Mix it in the mixture and serve instantly.

RECIPE #164: RISOTTO WITH COCKLES AND SHRIMPS

Preparation time: 30 minutes

Servings: 4-6

Ingredients:

- Olive oil as pre requirement
- 60 grams of chopped onions
- 2 zucchinis
- 80 grams' octopus
- 120 ml of white wine
- 4 cleaned shrimps
- Grated lemon
- Fish stock
- 4 spoons vanilla syrup
- 1 tablespoon cream
- 200 grams of Arborio rice
- 1 tablespoon of butter

Directions:

1. Take a pan add some olive oil in it add some butter and onion and fry it. After this add rice, wine and cook them gently until immersed.
2. Add zucchinis and stock. Cook the octopus and shrimps and stir it continuously until cooed.
3. Remove the mixture from flame and add cream, salt and vanilla syrup, and pepper in it. Then Serve it.

RECIPE #165: CUTTLEFISH RISOTTO

Preparation time: 30 minutes

Servings: 4

Ingredients:

- 1200 gram of cuttlefish
- olive oil as required
- 1200 gram of cuttlefish
- 280 gram of Arborio rice
- 20 grams of parsley
- 200 grams of chopped onion
- 60 grams of chopped tomatoes
- 20 grams of garlic clove
- Salt, pepper as required
- 1 tablespoon of butter.

Directions:

1. Take a pan and add olive oil in it add onion, garlic, and parsley, meat salt in the pan and allow it to fry.
2. Add tomatoes and black pepper, and allow it to cook for some time.
3. Add the rice and water and allow for rice to become softened.
4. In last add the 1 spoon of butter and serve it.

RECIPE #166: GARLIC PRAWNS

Preparation time: 10 minutes

Servings: 4

Ingredients:

- 450 grams of prawns
- 1tablespoon of chopped parsley
- olive oil as required
- 3 crushed cloves of garlic
- Red chilies, Black pepper, Salt according to taste

Directions:

1. Take a pan and add prawns with garlic paste in the pan. Add a small amount of pepper and parsley in it.
2. Fry the material till the color of prawns become pink.
3. Then pour it into the dish and serve it.

RECIPE #167: CRAB SALAD

Preparation time: 30 minutes

Servings: 4

Ingredients:

- 2 crabs
- 100 grams of crab flesh
- Pepper
- 2 onions
- 3 tablespoons of mayonnaise
- salt as required
- 1 chopped tomato
- 1 cup of wine
- 1garlic clove
- basil bunch
- herbs as required
- 1 lemon

Directions:

1. Take wine and herbs in a pan and allow it to boil add crabs in it.
2. Add the onions and garlic in a bowl adds olive oil, tomatoes, and basil in it. Add the boiled crabs in it and allow it to marinate.
3. Add a small amount of mayonnaise in it also add pepper to make it taste good.
4. Serve it with the bread.

RECIPE #168: STUFFED MUSHROOMS WITH PRAWNS IN A RED SWEET WINE SAUCE

Preparation time: 30 minutes

Servings: 8

Ingredients:

- 16 mushrooms
- 400 grams of prawns
- 2 chopped green onions
- 1 chopped leek
- 1 cup of cream
- 2 chopped zucchini
- half tablespoon of mint
- 1 chopped garlic clove
- olive oil as required
- cognac as required
- 2 tablespoons of chopped dill
- 1 cup of red wine
- half tablespoon of thyme

Directions:

1. Take a pan and add some olive oil in it add the salt, mushrooms, and pepper and allow them to fry for some time.
2. Fry the shells in olive oil add the cognac and salt and water in it.
3. Take another pot and fry the garlic, leek, and onions in it. Add prawns and zucchini in it. After this add the wine.
4. Add the prawns in the stuff of mushroom.
5. Serve it with sauce and cream.

RECIPE #169: STUFFED COURGETTE FLOWERS

Preparation time: 20minutes

Servings: 6

Ingredients:

- 800 grams of corvette flowers
- 300 green corvettes
- 200 grams of cheese
- Salt as required
- 1 lemon juice
- 100 grams of onions
- 1 tablespoon of parsley
- 150 grams of rice

- 2-3 tablespoon of olive oil

Directions:

1. Take a pan and add olive oil in it and add onions and corvettes in it.
2. Add the lemon juice, parsley, and feta cheese in it. After this add salt in it and fill the flower with the material.
3. Add water to a pan and the olive oil and allow it to boil at low temperature.
4. Then serve it.

RECIPE #170: STUFFED OCTOPUS

Preparation time: 30 minutes

Servings: 6-8

Ingredients:

- 2 kg of octopus
- 200 grams of trout
- 5 chopped onions
- 100 grams of ginger
- 2 chopped peppers
- 200 grams of mushrooms

- 2 cups of breadcrumbs
- 100 grams of ginger root
- 2 cups of wine
- 1 tablespoon of butter
- 4 tablespoons of parsley
- Black pepper to taste.

Directions:

1. Add onions, pepper, ginger, and breadcrumbs in a pot and add lemon juice and mushrooms.
2. Fry the mixture in the butter and add the mixture in octopus
3. Place the filled octopus in the oven and baked it for about 2 hours at about 170 degrees.
4. Then serve it.

RECIPE #171: DELICIOUS LOBSTER PASTA

Preparation time: 20 minutes

Servings: 6

Ingredients:

- 1 kilogram of lobster,
- 2 grated onions
- 1 dill bunch
- 1 and a half kilograms of chopped tomatoes

- Pepper, salt as required
- a half cup of olive oil
- half glass brandy
- a half kilogram of spaghetti

Directions:

1. Take a pan and olive oil in it, add the onions and tomatoes and mix it well with this add salt, pepper, and a water cup.
2. When the mixture becomes thickens add the brandy. After some time add the lobster.
3. Take another pan and add water and oil to it. Add the spaghetti to boil
4. Add the spaghetti to the lobster mixture and include the dill and add salt, pepper.
5. Then serve it.

RECIPE #172: FAN MUSSEL CROQUETTES/ RISSOLES

Preparation time: 20 minutes

Servings: 3-4

Ingredients:

- 1 chopped onion
- 1 Tablespoon of mint
- cup of flour
- 6 chopped mussels
- 1 egg
- 2 bread slices1

- 1 Tablespoon of trichinas
- Ouzo as required
- olive oil as required

Directions:

1. Add the trichinas, mussels chopped, onions, egg, mint, and ouzo in a bowl and leave the mixture to marinate for about half an hour.
2. Press the bread in the hand and add into the marinated mixture.
3. Make the ground balls or whatever shape you like and put into the flour.
4. Take a pan and add olive oil in it and fry the rolls or balls and serve it.

RECIPE #173: SHRIMP SOUP

Preparation time: 35 minutes

Servings: 4

Ingredients:

- 4 green onions
- 3 tablespoons of parsley
- 7 water glasses
- bay leaf
- 1 and a half kilogram of shrimp

- half tablespoon of pepper
- 1 and a half wine glass
- 1 tablespoon of salt
- 1 tablespoon of thyme
- Juice of 1 lemon

Directions:

1. Take a pot and add water, parsley, and wine in it, add shrimps in it.
2. Remove from fire and remove the skin from shrimp. Add scallions and parsley and pepper.
3. Sprinkle the lemon juice and serve it.

RECIPES #174: OUZO WITH SEAFOOD AND FETA

Preparation time: 20 minutes

Servings: 4-5

Ingredients:

- 10 scallops
- 10 prawns
- 1 chopped tomato
- olive oil as required
- 100 grams' cheese
- 1 garlic clove

- 1 chopped onions
- 2 tablespoon of chopped parsley
- ouzo, pepper, salt as required

Directions:

1. Take a pan and add salt to it. Add olive oil and add scallops in it and fry for about 3 minutes. After this add prawns.
2. Add the ouzo, onions and garlic paste and add tomatoes and cheese.
3. When the cheese starts melting, add parsley and serve it.

RECIPE #175: SAVARIN OF RICE WITH SCAMPI TAILS

Preparation time: 40 minutes

Servings: 4

Ingredients:

- 150 grams of rice
- Water as required
- 1chopped onion
- bay leaf
- 2 garlic cloves
- 1 carrot
- olive oil

- semolina
- 20 scampi
- 1 beet
- 1 parsnip
- 1 zucchini
- lobster sauce
- 1 tablespoon of peas

Directions:

1. Take a pan add onions, cloves, and bay leaf in it. Add the clean rice in it and add water to it.
2. Add the vegetables to it and also add butter.
3. Fry the scampi in olive oil for decoration.
4. Take the sauce in the plate and serve it with warm rice.

RECIPE #176: BREADED CRAWFISH WITH SPICES

Preparation time: 30 minutes

Servings: 6

Ingredients:

- 20 slices of baguette
- 20 cleaned crawfish
- 5 slices of bread
- orange gratings
- parsley bunch
- olive oil
- salt as required

- pepper

Directions:

1. Blend the bread with the orange gratings and parsley leaves.
2. Apply this mixture on crawfish and fry it in the olive oil. Add pepper and salt.
3. Serve them with the bread.

RECIPE#177: SPICY OCTOPUS

Preparation time: 40 minutes

Servings: 4

Ingredients:

- 1 kilogram of octopus
- 1tablespoon of black pepper
- 1 tablespoon of chopped ginger
- 1 tablespoon of red pepper
- 1 tablespoon of allspice
- 1 tablespoon of cumin
- Pinch of cinnamon
- 1 tablespoon of green pepper
- 1 tablespoon of black peppercorns
- 1 tablespoon of allspice

- 1 tablespoon of cloves
- 1 tablespoon of thyme
- 1 tablespoon of marjoram
- 1 tablespoon of rosemary
- 3 tablespoons of butter
- 3 tablespoons of brandy

Directions:

1. Preheat the oven and align the octopus in a dish and sprinkle all the ingredients in equal proportion as mentioned above.
2. Keep it in the oven at a suitable temperature for about one and half hour until the thick liquid appears.

RECIPE #178: ALMOND PISTACHIO BAKLAVA

Preparation time: 35 minutes

Servings: 4

Ingredients:

- Water as required
- 4 sugar cups
- 2 tablespoons lemon juice
- Honey
- 4 unsalted cups pistachios
- 1 and a half tablespoon of cinnamon
- Half tablespoon nutmeg
- 1cup of butter
- filo pastry (3 packs)
- 3 cups almonds

Directions:

1. Take a pan, add water, sugar, lemon, and honey and boil it.
2. Take a blender and put nuts for grinding and then add sugar, nutmeg, and cinnamon.
3. Put butter in the pan and mix pastry.

4. Add the pastry to the bottom of a pan.

5. Make almost 14 layers of pastry and add a small proportion of nuts to it.

6. Repeat the procedure and make almost 14 layers.

7. Make different pieces, bake for 40 minutes in an oven to almost 350F.

8. Then cool it and pour sugar liquid on it, cover it.

RECIPE#179: NESTED BERRIES

Preparation time: 20 minutes

Servings:4-6

Ingredients:

- Four cups strawberries
- Blackberries (1 cup)
- Raspberries (1 cup)
- Sugar (1/2 cup)
- 3tablespoon of vinegar
- Filo pastry (8 sheets)
- Half tablespoon black pepper
- 2tablespoon sugar
- Quarter tablespoon cinnamon
- Filo nests

Directions:

1. Add the berries in a bowl and add sugar, vinegar, and pepper over it.
2. Prepare a muffin tray and unfold filo pastry. Add the sugar and the cinnamon and add the dough to it.
3. Repeat the process to make another one
4. Bake the dough when it becomes brownish.
5. Remove it from the oven and serve it.

RECIPE#180: TIRAMISU

Preparation time: 35 minutes

Servings: 12

Ingredients:

- 6 egg
- 4 cups of cheese
- 1 cup of milk
- chocolate (Bittersweet)
- sugar
- 1and a half cup of coffee
- Half cup brandy
- cocoa powder
- 32 lady fingers

Directions:

1. Take a bowl and blend the eggs, sugar and milk together until it becomes homogenous. Heat the bowl.

2. Take a bowl and mix the coffee and dunk the ladyfingers in it. Make the custard mascarpone and spread it on the layer of ladyfinger.

3. Make the layers of the custard and add ladyfingers until the mixture is finished.

4. Sprinkle the cocoa powder over it.

5. Wrap with the plastic cover and keep in refrigerator.

6. Then serve it.

RECIPE #181: WHITE CHOCOLATE CUPS WITH DARK CHOCOLATE AND MASCARPONE

Preparation time: 40 minutes

Servings: 8

Ingredients:

- 8oz of chopped chocolate (white)
- 4oz of chopped chocolate (dark)
- 3 tablespoons of sugar
- 8oz (mascarpone) cheese
- vanilla extract
- 1 tablespoon of grated orange peel
- whipping cream

- white chocolate for decoration

Directions:

1. Take a pan and melt the white chocolate. Place a liner in muffin cups and pour 1 tablespoon of white chocolate over it.
2. Put it in the freezer.
3. Again apply the melted dark chocolate over the paper and put in the freezer for almost 1 an hour.
4. Blend the cream and sugar in a bowel. Wisk the mascarpone in the bowel with dark chocolate, vanilla, and orange peels.
5. Add the cream over the mascarpone and add chocolate. Then serve it.

RECIPE #182: FLORENTINES

Preparation time: 45 minutes

Servings: 28 cookies

Ingredients:

- 1 cup of sliced almonds,
- Salt
- 2 tablespoons of corn syrup
- 2 tablespoons of cream
- Half tablespoon of vanilla extract

- 1 grated orange
- 3 tablespoons of flour
- 5 tablespoons of unsalted butter
- 4oz of chopped dark chocolate.
- sugar

Directions:

1. Blend the almond. Mix the salt, flour, and nuts in a bowl.
2. Take a frying pan and add sugar, cream, butter, and corn and heat it until the sugar dissolve.
3. After this add the vanilla extract and add the cream mixture to the almond mixture.
4. Wait for some time so that the mixture gets homogenous. Make the small balls and put it on the baking paper.
5. Bake the mixture for about 9 minutes.
6. Pour the chocolate on the smooth side of a cookie and join together, with the other one.
7. Put it in the fridge. Serve the cookies with chocolate.

RECIPE #183: HOMEMADE RICE PUDDING

Preparation time: 25 minutes

Servings:4

Ingredients:

- White rice (1cup)
- 5 water cups
- 2 cinnamon sticks
- 1 can of condensed milk
- 1 can of evaporated milk
- 1 cup of milk
- Half cup raisins
- Grounded cinnamon

Directions:

1. Take a pan and add water, sticks of cinnamon and rice. Boil it until the rice becomes soft.
2. Remove from flame and take out the cinnamon stick.
3. In a bowl add condensed, evaporated milk and whole milk.
4. Add the milk to the rice jar and cook for about 20 minutes.
5. Add the raisins and stir continuously and serve it.

RECIPE #184: EASY FRENCH CREPES

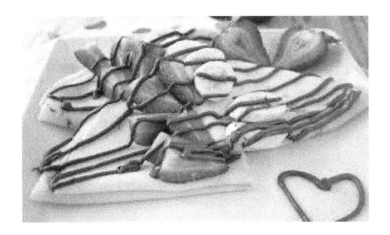

Preparation time: 5 minutes

Servings: 12

Ingredients:

- 1tablespoon of sugar
- Salt as required
- 2 eggs
- Fresh fruits
- 1tablespoon of butter
- 1 and a half cup of milk
- icing sugar
- Flour 1 cup

Directions:

1. Add flour, salt and the sugar cup in a bowl
2. Add the milk and egg and start beating. Leave it for some time.
3. Take frying pan, apply some butter and pour the paste over it and allow it to cook for some time.
4. Repeat the process to make another one.
5. Serve it with the fruits and icing sugar at the top.

RECIPE #185: PAN ROASTED ALMONDS WITH HONEY

Preparation time: 10 minutes

Servings: 08

Ingredients:

- Water as required
- 4 tablespoon of honey
- 1 cup of almonds

Directions:

1. Take a pot and add water to it then boil it.
2. Add almonds to the boiled water. Remove the skin of almond.
3. Dessert making process:
4. Take a pan and add honey to it after that add the almonds and cook it at a low temperature.
5. After it becomes brown remove the flame.
6. Pour the mixture into the bowls and serve it.

RECIPE #186: HONEY DONUTS—LOUKOUMADES

Preparation time: 10 minutes

Servings: 25

Ingredients:

- 3 and a half cups flour
- Yeast pack
- warm water
- 1 tablespoon of salt
- sugar
- milk cup
- 2 eggs
- 32oz oil of safflower
- cinnamon
- nuts

Directions:

1. Take a bowl and add milk, egg, salt, flour, yeast, and water in it.
2. Cover the material and after some time adds honey and water to it.
3. Add the safflower oil in the pan and heat it.
4. Take a mixture and pour it into the oil until turn golden.
5. Place all the donuts on the plate and serve it with the syrup.

RECIPE #187: MOZAIK PASTASI

Preparation time: 30 minutes

Servings: 6

Ingredients:

- 2 packs of biscuits
- 1 cup of melted butter
- 1 tablespoon of vanilla extract
- 3oz of melted dark chocolate

Sugar

- half cup cocoa powder
- 4 eggs

Directions:

1. Take a bowl and add sugar, cocoa powder, butter, chocolate, and vanilla extract in it and stir well.
2. Add the egg and beat them gently to make a homogenous mixture.
3. Add the broken biscuits in another bowl and pour the mixture over it.
4. Add the mixture to the pan. Allow the mixture to cool well for some time.

RECIPE #188: MOROCCAN ORANGE CAKE

Preparation time: 20 minutes

Servings:4-6

Ingredients:

- 4 eggs
- Flour 2 cups
- 1 and a half cup of sugar
- Half cup vegetable oil
- 2 tablespoons of orange zest
- Half tablespoon of salt
- 1 tablespoon of vanilla extract
- 4 tablespoons of baking powder
- Half cup orange juice

Directions:

1. Take a bowl and beat the egg add sugar in it.
2. Add the orange juice, baking powder, salt, and flour in a bowl and beat well until it becomes smooth.
3. After this add vanilla extract and continue beating. Pour the whole liquid into the pan and allow it to bake for about 45 minutes.
4. Allow it to cool for, about 10 minutes.

RECIPE#189: BASIL & PISTACHIO PESTO

Preparation time: 5minutes

Servings: 4

Ingredients:

- shelled pistachios
- 3 cloves of garlic
- 60 grams of washed basil
- 1 lime juice
- olive oil

Directions:

1. Blend all the ingredients in a bowl.
2. Place in the refrigerator in different portions.
3. Then serve it.

RECIPE#190: CINNAMON STRAWS

Preparation time: 15 minutes

Servings: 24

Ingredients:

- 4 cups of sugar
- 4 teaspoons of cinnamon
- 5 tablespoons of butter

- Frozen puff pastry sheets

Directions:

1. Mix the sugar, cinnamon in a bowl.
2. Take a pastry sheet and add 1 tablespoon of oil to the sheet. Smoothly pour the cinnamon on a sheet. Cut the sheet into 10 equal pieces.
3. Melt the butter and apply on the strips.
4. Bake the strips until the color change.

RECIPE #191: MEDITERRANEAN PISTACHIOS AND FRUITS

Preparation time: 15 minutes

Servings: 4

Ingredients:

- 1 and a half cup of pistachios
- Dried pomegranate seeds
- Half cup of chopped dried apricot
- Grounded allspice
- Grounded nutmeg
- cinnamon

- sugar

Directions:

1. Pour the pistachios on a baking sheet and bake it until fried.
2. Add apricots, nutmeg, allspice, cinnamon, pomegranate seeds and sugar on pistachios.
3. Then serve it.

RECIPES#192: FRENCH PEAR TART

Preparation time: 16 minutes

Servings: 4

Ingredients:

- 1 and a half cup of flour
- 5 tablespoons of sugar
- Half teaspoon of salt
- 12 tablespoons of melted butter (unsalted)
- 8 large pears
- water

- fig jam
- salt

Directions:

1. Add the sugar, salt, and flour in a bowl.
2. Melt the butter and add to the mixture.
3. Add the mixture to the pan. Bake it until the mixture turn golden brown.
4. Add the fig jam and slices of pears.
5. Melt the butter adds the pear and water and cook for about 5 minutes.
6. Cut the pear to a small size and apply it to the mixture.
7. Heat the mixture into the oven and apply butter on the pears.
8. Then serve it.

RECIPE #193: S'MORES COOKIE BARS

Preparation time: 55 minutes

Servings: 4

Ingredients:

- 2 cups of flour
- Salt as required
- 2 cups of crushed crumbs
- 1 and a half cup of brown sugar

- 2 cups of marshmallows
- Butter
- 1 teaspoon of baking powder
- 1 teaspoon of vanilla extract
- 2 eggs
- 2 cups of chocolate chips milk

Directions:

1. Mix the cup of flour, cracker, crumbs, baking powder and salt in a bowl.
2. Beat the butter and add sugar in it. After this add the mixture to the butter and sugar paste. Divide the mixture into two equal parts.
3. Make the cookie base add marshmallow and spread the mixture over it. Add the chocolate chips.
4. Add the remaining dough at the top of the mixture. Bake the mixture until turns golden brown.
5. Then serve it.

RECIPE#194: SANGRIA ICE POPS

Preparation time: 15 minutes

Servings:4-6

Ingredients:

- 250 milliliter of pomegranate juice
- 60 milliliter of syrup
- 2 chopped apples
- 2 chopped ripe pears
- 2 tablespoons of corn syrup
- 750-milliliters of red wine
- 2 tablespoons of orange juice
- 2 tablespoons of grape juice
- 2 chopped orange

Directions:

- Mix the orange juice, grape juice, chopped orange, pears and apple in a bowl.
- Keep the mixture in the refrigerator.

RECIPE#195: GRIDDLED HONEY-ORANGE FIGS WITH MASCARPONE AND PISTACHIOS

Preparation time: 10 minutes

Servings:6

Ingredients

- 4 tablespoons of honey
- 60 milliliter of orange juice
- 12 pieces of figs
- Soaked skewers
- 500 grams of mascarpone
- 30 grams of chopped pistachios.

Directions:

1. Take a bowl and add honey and orange juice stir it until completely mixed. Apply the orange mixture over the fig.
2. Add the honey and chopped pistachios and serve.

RECIPE#196: FRESH FRUIT PLATTER

Preparation time: 15 minutes

Servings: 10-12

Ingredients:

- 2 melons
- 1 pineapple
- 1 papaya

- 225 gram of blueberries
- 225 grams of figs
- 225 grams of raspberries
- 225 grams of strawberries
- 2 grapes bunches

Directions:

1. Make a base with the help of melon, pineapple. Add figs, raspberries, strawberries, and grapes.
2. Use leaves of grapes, figs, and lemon to cover the side of the bowl with green leaves.
3. Then serve it.

RECIPE#197: CHOUX PASTRY DELIGHTS

Preparation time: 40 minutes

Servings: 6

Ingredients:

- 200 ml of fresh cream
- 175 ml of water
- 150 ml of crème Fraiche
- 75 grams of butter
- 110 grams of flour
- 3 eggs

- Salt as required
- 200 grams of dark chopped chocolate
- Honey
- 150 grams of mascarpone cheese
- Icing sugar
- 1 chopped orange
- 200 grams of raspberries
- 6 strawberries

Directions:

1. Mix the flour and salt.
2. Add the water to a pan and allow it to boil after this adds butter in it. Add the flour to the mixture and beat well.
3. Again place the pan on the flame and cook for some time. After this add egg and beat them well.
4. Bake this mixture into the oven for about 30 minutes. The color will change into golden brown.
5. Mix the cream with the chocolate in the pan and stir well and place it on the stove for about one minute.
6. Add mascarpone to the bowl add orange zest, honey, as required.
7. Make the pastry half and fill with the raspberries also add mascarpone mixture.
8. Then serve it.

RECIPE#199: CHOCOLATE AND BANANA CREPES

Preparation time: 15 minutes

Servings:6-8

Ingredients:

- One and half cups milk
- One cup flour
- Two tablespoons of sugar
- One tablespoon vanilla
- Salt as required
- Butter (Quarter cup)
- Two bananas
- Three eggs
- Melted chocolate (Half cup)

Directions:

1. Mix milk, flour, sugar, butter, eggs, salt, and vanilla in a blender and shake until it becomes smooth.
2. Take a Pan and put it on the stove with medium heat coated with butter.
3. Add batter to pan and cook it for about 2 minutes, until bubbles are formed, then flip it and again cook for 1 min.
4. Repeat procedure with remaining batter then place crepes on to the plate
5. Overlay crepes into quarters also with banana cuts
6. Sprinkle it with melted chocolate, it is ready.

RECIPE#199: HOMEMADE CREPE CAKE

Preparation time: 15 minutes

Servings: 6-8

Ingredients:

- Milk (2 cups)
- One and half cups flour
- ¾ tablespoon salt
- 1/3 a cup sugar
- 5tablespoon butter
- 6 eggs
- Chocolate pudding (3 cups)
- 1tablespoon sugar

Directions:

1. Mix flour, salt, eggs, and sugar in bowl
2. Pour down the mixture into milk and whisk it fully.
3. Mix it in butter and wait for some time.
4. Add batter to the pan and cook it for almost half an hour with flipping.
5. Put the crepe on plate, cover it with wax paper. Make 20 more.
6. Put crepe on plate and spread chocolate pudding on it
7. Sprinkle sugar.

Conclusion

Get the delicious food varieties for your everyday meal with this tremendous and superb guide for the Mediterranean food. This cookbook includes the amazing and easiest food items which vary greatly as per your taste and your demand. You can use any of these recipes for the next whole year and avail the chance of having incredibly yummiest, low fat and healthful meals.